"Filled with self-directed, age-appropriate enrichment projects that _____ of challenge. Includes everything a teacher needs, including material lists, student responsibilities, and authentic, performance-based assessment tools."
—*Curriculum Administrator*

"A great resource for teachers looking to offer advanced learning opportunities. Filled with self-enrichment projects that teach middle and high school students to go beyond the core curriculum by researching topics in zoology, astronomy, current events, or even sports statistics. Recommended for math, social studies, and science instruction."
—North Carolina Department of Public Instruction

Challenging
PROJECTS
FOR CREATIVE MINDS

20 Self-Directed Enrichment Projects that Develop and Showcase Student Ability

for Grades 6 and Up

by Phil Schlemmer, M.Ed., and Dori Schlemmer

Edited by Caryn Pernu

free spirit
PUBLiSHiNG®

Works
for kids®

Library of Congress Cataloging-in-Publication Data

Challenging projects for creative minds : 20 self-directed enrichment projects that develop and showcase student ability for grades 6 and up / by Phil Schlemmer and Dori Schlemmer ; edited by Caryn Pernu.

p. cm.

Includes bibliographical references and index

ISBN 1-57542-049-X

1. Education, Elementary—Activity programs. 2. Education, Secondary—Activity programs. 3. Project method in teaching. 4. Creative activities and seat work. 5. Independent study. 6. Curriculum enrichment.

I. Schlemmer, Phil. II. Schlemmer, Dori. III. Pernu, Caryn.

LB1592.C53   1998

372.13′6—dc21

98-36262

CIP

Cover design by Circus

Book design and typesetting by Percolator

Illustrations by Marty Harris

Index compiled by Diana Witt

10 9 8 7 6 5 4

Printed in the United States of America

Free Spirit Publishing Inc.

217 Fifth Avenue North, Suite 200

Minneapolis, MN 55401-1299

(612) 338-2068

help4kids@freespirit.com

www.freespirit.com

Dedication

To the millions of kids across America who are trusting the adults in their lives to prepare them for a demanding, unpredictable future world, and to the teachers who work to fulfill that trust.

Acknowledgments

We wish to thank the many students and educators who have provided valuable input over the years as these materials were developed. Their insights, discoveries, and affirmations were helpful in designing a program that works on many levels.

Contents

Section 3: Project Forms and Resources

117

Preface

Most people accept that students today need to adapt to a rapidly changing world. But how do students become self-directed and motivated learners? How do they learn to solve problems, look at issues in new ways, authentically practice the knowledge and skills that teachers try to pass on?

To develop the critical skills for making sense of the world, to become true learners, students need *structure* coupled with *freedom*. Structure establishes well-defined guidelines, clear expectations, and a supportive environment. Freedom allows students to make informed decisions and choices about their learning. Because people continue learning throughout their lives, they need opportunities to study areas that fit their needs and interests and to develop their personal strengths. Students also need to learn strategies that will enable them to find relevant information, think critically, and transform knowledge into something they can use for a specific purpose. This book of performance-based projects offers a systematic way to provide students both the structure and the freedom to become actively engaged in their own learning.

First published as *Merit Projects* (Learning to Learn Company, 1994), the projects in this book have been used in a wide variety of ways, in schools across the United States. With this publication, *Challenging Projects for Creative Minds* incorporates feedback from students and teachers who have used these projects. It provides twenty fully developed projects and the organizational structure needed to make them work in your school and with your students.

While the materials were originally designed for gifted and talented students, schools have been using them successfully with students of many abilities and interests. All students have talents and need the opportunity to develop them to their fullest potential; these projects set the stage for that development. By taking ownership of a project from start to finish and sharing what they've done with others, students often accomplish more than they dreamed possible. They may even discover abilities they didn't know they had.

The world is changing so fast, it's difficult to see around the corners. Things don't always work. And when they don't work, what you can fall back on is talent.

—Charles Fishman

Teachers and schools grapple with the question "What will our students need to know and be able to do as they enter adulthood?" Although we all make guesses, no one really knows. We don't know what career opportunities will be available, what technologies will be current, what information will be critical, what skills will be in demand, or what an unpredictable and ever-changing world will require of its citizens. For example, in 1990, who would have predicted that the Internet would have a significant impact on students' everyday lives? One thing is abundantly clear: Today's students will need to learn and grow throughout their lives. People who dedicate themselves to learning how to learn will be ready for the inevitable changes that will affect their lives.

At first glance, some might think that the learning-to-learn philosophy holds that *content,* or *what students learn,* is irrelevant—that only skills and strategies are important. Nothing could be further from the truth.

Content forms the foundation of every project in this book. Rather than providing lessons on the specific topics, the projects guide students in their quest for information and help them create a context for it. Students research facts, analyze their findings, develop complex strategies for synthesizing the information, and finally share what they've learned with others. By becoming intimately involved with the subject matter, learners not only internalize and remember what they've studied, but they also gain a universal set of tools for working with information, tools they can use throughout their lives.

In every sphere of study, knowledge is expanding at dizzying rates. A whole new world of information has become more accessible to more people. The key to tapping into this knowledge is learning how to find the relevant information and put it to use. We all need current information to do our jobs effectively. Who wants to go to a doctor who doesn't keep up with recent medical discoveries and treatments? Would you take your new computerized car to a mechanic who isn't familiar with the latest technologies?

Schools can't provide all the facts and information students need in their lives, but they can teach students how to find what they need to know and how to use that information. To do this, schools don't have to change what they teach, but they do need to give students an increasingly active and responsible role in working with information.

the potential for any of these projects to be supported or enhanced with technology.

Because *Challenging Projects* is designed to be used by any teacher in any classroom in any school, most of the projects don't require computers. While some teachers will naturally use technology without prompting, teachers who either don't have equipment available or aren't inclined to employ it will avoid projects that seem to require its use. For example, "Moments in Time" asks the student to create a paper time line. Any teacher with access to general reference materials and some empty wall space can offer the project to students. Computer-savvy teachers, however, know instinctively that technology offers numerous ways to enhance the project: everything from using research resources such as CD-ROM databases and the Internet, to producing hyper-linked multimedia time lines on the Web, to word-processing reports and brochures.

Because technology resources are so diverse and access to equipment varies incredibly from school to school, we've simply defined the expected learner outcomes for these projects and left it to teachers and students to decide how, and to what extent, to apply available tools of technology. Most of the projects have no specific technology requirements; you can, however, easily and appropriately incorporate technology into every project in the book. It is entirely up to you and the kids in your school.

A Word About Technology

Challenging Projects for Creative Minds provides many opportunities to use technology in the classroom. If you or your school places a premium on technology-based student demonstrations, then you will immediately recognize

Check It Out

Learning with Technology edited by Chris Dede (Alexandria, Va.: ASCD, 1998). This yearbook discusses a vision of education in the twenty-first century, including ways to use technology to empower and extend learning communities.

How to Use This Book

Because *Challenging Projects for Creative Minds* provides the structure and choice that students need to work independently, there is an inherent flexibility in how schools can implement the program. Schools or classroom teachers may decide to:

1. offer the projects as extensions or enrichment opportunities within each classroom,

2. include projects as part of the regular curriculum, or

3. set up a special program for gifted or highly motivated students.

Some schools that use this program require each student to complete a project for a high-school graduation portfolio. However you decide to use these projects, students gain the most when the school establishes clear guidelines and recognizes students who achieve the goals.

This book is divided into three sections:

Section 1:
Using Challenging Projects
for Creative Minds

This section gives educators an overview of the program. It details the goals and organization, the students' and teachers' responsibilities, and assessment. It also discusses using the projects for small-group work, and describes in detail how to write original projects using the teaching philosophy behind the projects in this book.

Section 2:
Student Projects

This section offers students an overview of the program and contains all twenty project assignments and guidelines.

Section 3:
Project Forms and Resources

Reproducible materials guide students in choosing and planning a project, reporting their progress and problems, recording their resources and work time, and assessing the project. Other forms help teachers write new projects and clarify assessment expectations.

Check It Out

Much of this book is reproducible—including all of the project assignments, assessments, and forms. When reproducing materials for your students to use, be sure to read through the introduction and assignment to make sure you've included all the pages they will need.

Using Challenging Projects for Creative Minds

Introduction

Educators work hard to meet the needs of their students. The average classroom today serves students with a broad range of learning needs and instructional challenges. Students come to school with extraordinary talents, learning disabilities, a wide variety of personal interests, disparate background knowledge, different levels of motivation, and different goals. How can schools serve highly capable learners, motivate all students, and equip children with skills that will help them learn throughout their lifetime? Obviously, there aren't easy answers, but the projects in this book are designed to help schools meet these challenges.

Challenging Projects for Creative Minds is based on the concept of authentic learning. This means that students learn from assignments that provide a relevant, "real world" experience and personally engage them in learning. Rather than relying on worksheets or paper-and-pencil assignments, students become actively involved in gathering new information, building on their existing knowledge, and connecting this knowledge with the world outside the classroom. Authentic learning requires students to use a wide range of resources, activities, skills, and strategies. The projects in this book tap into this idea. Each has a scenario that gives students a true-to-life role to play and a reason for doing their best work. For example, a student working on a project may act as an athletic specialist who develops a training program for young athletes, an illustrator who designs a cover for a classic book, or a team member producing a new television series for teens.

The goal of *Challenging Projects* is to provide opportunities for students to explore the topics that interest *them* by completing in-depth projects. Typically, whether working alone or in small groups, students select a project, define a specific topic that will help them meet personal learning goals, set due dates and presentation plans, and then work to complete the project under the guidance of a teacher. Step-by-step assignments and assessment forms ensure that both teachers and students understand exactly what's expected; yet every completed project is unique because of the many decisions and choices students make to develop the assignment around their interests, aptitudes, and knowledge.

Meeting Student Needs

The student projects in this book are designed with flexibility in mind to help develop a broad range of skills and intelligences among students. The theory of *multiple intelligences,* described by Howard Gardner*, stresses the idea that intelligence is not a single domain but a collection of independent factors that we all possess in degrees that vary from person to person. Gardner currently identifies eight intelligences:

Verbal-linguistic intelligence. People who are strong in this intelligence are highly verbal. They are good at activities that involve language: reading, writing, talking, poetry.

Logical-mathematical intelligence. People who think logically or mathematically are keenly

---

Frames of Mind: The Theory of Multiple Intelligences (New York: Basic Books, 1993) describes seven intelligences. Dr. Gardner announced his conceptualization of an eighth intelligence—naturalist—at a national conference in June 1995.

aware of numbers and patterns. They gravitate toward activities that involve abstract reasoning, mathematics, science, computers, or debate.

Visual-spatial intelligence. People with visual-spatial intelligence are extremely good at tasks that involve seeing, visualizing, or manipulating lines and objects. They excel at art, science, chess, puzzles, or tasks that require hand-eye coordination.

Musical-rhythmic intelligence. People with developed musical intelligence can easily recognize musical themes, pitch, tone, and rhythm. They are naturally inclined toward composing, singing, instrumental music, rhythm, and sound.

Bodily-kinesthetic intelligence. People who have bodily-kinesthetic intelligence show an enormous capacity for whole-body or fine-motor control. They gravitate toward athletics, dance, acting, crafts, inventing, and active learning.

Interpersonal intelligence. People with interpersonal intelligence have well developed social skills. They tend to be attuned to other people's moods, motivations, and intentions. Their strengths include group work, leadership, mediation, and organizing others.

Intrapersonal intelligence. People with intrapersonal intelligence have a high level of insight and awareness of their own strengths, emotions, and goals. They tend to be goal-oriented, independent, and self-directed, preferring to learn alone rather than in a group activity.

Naturalist intelligence. Some people have an innate affinity for the natural world. They thrive on working with plants and animals, categorizing and sorting the world around them.

Most people tend to be stronger in one or two of these areas, although everyone has a blend of abilities among these intelligences. By offering a wide variety of options for students to demonstrate what they know and can do, teachers set the stage for students to develop and apply their intelligences.

Challenging Projects for Creative Minds has an open-ended design so that students can work within their most comfortable areas of intelligence or branch out and develop other areas. Students naturally tend to choose projects and presentation formats that highlight their strongest abilities. For example, students with strong visual-spatial intelligence may gravitate toward projects that call for an artistic presentation (such as "Express Yourself"), while those with developed naturalist intelligence would more likely lean toward "Menagerie from the Mind," which calls for classifying imaginary plants and animals. Students will find that many projects combine aspects of the different intelligences, and that they can create ways to use their special talents in just about any project.

Providing students challenging opportunities to develop strengths, skills, and the confidence to learn independently prepares them for an ever-changing world. Students learn to think critically, analyze problems, find information, identify solutions, cope with setbacks, and demonstrate what they learn. Students can take responsibility for their own education. They can, and must be allowed to, think for themselves.

Goals

Because these projects are based on sound principles of learning, you'll find that they can support the educational goals of both students and schools—whether the projects are used in an individual classroom, as a special enrichment opportunity, or as a schoolwide program.

*Using this program allows **STUDENTS** to:*

1. Direct their own learning by choosing enriching projects that they find interesting and valuable.

2. Develop practical and critical-thinking skills that they can apply to all areas of learning throughout their lives.

3. Develop self-confidence through completing a project that requires planning, problem solving, self-discipline, self-assessment, creativity, and public presentation.

4. Build a working knowledge of a topic that they explore in great depth.

5. Develop ownership of their learning as they set and achieve personal goals.

6. Discover new abilities and interests and practice skills.

7. Discuss their learning experiences and goals with other students and adults, including family members, school staff, and others in the community.

8. Develop a capacity for self-reflection and metacognition as they look back on their project and process what they've learned.

9. Present their projects to an audience and receive public recognition for their work.

10. Receive credit for their work in a way that fits their own learning goals.

*Using this program allows **SCHOOLS** to:*

1. Offer all students enrichment opportunities based on their motivation to participate.

2. Recognize and reward students' academic effort and achievement.

3. Offer students choice and variety in their education.

4. Give teachers opportunities to build extensions from the core curriculum. Teachers can let students pursue topics that are impossible to cover in regular coursework because of time constraints.

5. Increase or enhance use of educational resources such as:

- spare class time (for students who complete assignments early)
- after-school, weekend, and vacation study time
- media center facilities, faculty, and resources
- technology (computers, software, Internet, audio-video equipment)
- community resources, including libraries, businesses, and colleges
- student motivation
- untapped student potential
- basic skills and knowledge from the core curriculum

6. Involve parents in their child's education.

7. Showcase student abilities and achievements within both the school and the community.

8. Meet the needs of diverse learners.

9. Give students credit for high-quality work in a way that meets your school's needs.

Organizing a Program in Your School

The projects in this book are flexible enough in design that schools can use them in the way that best suits their needs and the needs of their students, whether it's in individual classrooms, as cross-curricular opportunities for teams, or in a schoolwide program.

Individual Classrooms

Many classroom teachers use the projects as enrichment opportunities for motivated students. These teachers work with students to develop a personal plan for learning and advise them in completing a project. Students discover fun and challenging opportunities to explore areas of personal interest and skills beyond the regular curriculum.

Other teachers sometimes assign a project to their entire class as part of the regular curriculum. For example, a history teacher might assign "Moments in Time" during a unit on early American history, asking each student to create a time line on a specific topic. One student might choose to study the Lewis and Clark expedition, another might choose to depict the events and meetings that led to the signing of the Declaration of Independence, and another might choose to show the changes that took place in the lives of Native Americans as settlers immigrated to North America. Students present their completed time lines to the class, sharing what they've learned with their peers. These projects can become the basis for an infinite variety of learning opportunities.

Cross-Curricular Teams

Challenging Projects for Creative Minds can also offer innovative ways of spanning curriculum boundaries. Language arts or mathematics teachers may team up with music or physical-education teachers to offer students special hands-on activities that meet objectives in both curricular areas. "Honored Athlete" combines both physical education and mathematics, for example, and "It's Written in the Stars" combines astronomy with composition. Also, because the projects and skills that students need to complete them aren't subject-specific, students can combine their interests in unique ways. One creative student integrated a civics research project with a class on HTML to create a multimedia presentation on prejudice and discrimination.

Schoolwide Enrichment

Incorporating these projects into a school-wide program offers the greatest benefits to the most students. It tells students, parents, and the community that their school promotes learning excellence and offers all students a shot at doing something special. Seeing projects that other students have completed helps instill pride in the school's academic achievements. And the effects can snowball. Students who recognize and congratulate the successes of fellow students become inspired by each other's creativity. The goal becomes not just a grade, but an experience.

The key to success for any schoolwide program is organizing it to support existing educational goals and communicating clearly with everyone involved. Schools that establish a system everyone understands are able to minimize confusion and maximize participation in the program. Each year, the program improves as you better define the structure and implementation and as students and staff become more aware of its benefits. As students see the incredible work their classmates have done, more will want to be involved in the program.

How Does the Program Work?

The guidelines suggested here describe setting up a basic schoolwide program, but they also apply generally to teachers who use it in their individual classrooms. Keep in mind that you can modify the program to address specific needs or use resources in your classroom, school, or community.

Who Can Participate?

Make *Challenging Projects* available to all students. Rather than trying to define methods for identifying worthy students, use student motivation as the basis for entering the program. Students who want to participate fill out a Project Request Form (see page 120) and get it approved by a supervising teacher before beginning work. Students who aren't motivated are unlikely to undertake a project.

Who Administers the Program?

To pilot the program schoolwide, select a team of supervising teachers to publicize and run the program. The team makes sure students, staff, and families are aware of the program and its goals. Team members organize the program within the school, explain the sign-up process to students and their families, and ensure that resources are available for students. They find ways to communicate with parents about the program to let them know it's available to their children. School newsletters, the school Web site, parent-teacher conferences—all offer opportunities to inform parents. Supervising teachers also serve as mentors or guides for the students, helping them fulfill the project requirements. Supervising teachers meet with students at the beginning of their projects to discuss individual plans and again as needed to help students stay on track.

How Does a Supervising Teacher Facilitate a Project?

In general, the supervising teacher will:

1. Sign the Project Request Form, giving the student formal approval to begin a project.

2. Set up a meeting to discuss the student's plans and to distribute the Project Packet, which includes all the necessary forms for the project (see page 8).

3. Be available as an advisor when a student needs help. Guide students through unfamiliar skills, point them to other sources of information, and offer encouragement and support.

4. Initiate regular meetings to check on progress and offer help if it is needed.

5. Meet with the student to discuss the Midproject Report (see pages 133–134) and ensure that the project is moving along.

6. Terminate a project that is not taken seriously or that is not being completed.

7. Attend the student's final presentation and assess the finished project.

8. Discuss the student's self-assessment of the finished project with the student.

9. Fill out a Certificate of Completion (see page 147) or a Certificate of Merit (see page 148) for the student, and present it at the recognition ceremony.

10. Record the student's project in his or her permanent file.

How Do Students Select Projects and Sign Up?

Making students aware that the program exists is only the first step in getting students involved. One way to encourage students to participate is to give them as much information about the program as possible, and to let their parents know about it as well. When students become interested and excited about doing a project, their parents are likely to be enthusiastic, too. Supervising teachers should keep several copies of *Challenging Projects for Creative Minds* in the media center or classroom for students to check out, along with Project Request Forms. When students take the book of projects home with them, parents can become actively involved in helping their children choose projects, and students become more thoughtful about making a final project selection. Many schools have been pleasantly surprised at the level of parent support and enthusiasm that comes from seeing the range of project options being offered to their children.

Once students select a project, they must formally request permission to work on it by filling out a Project Request Form (see page 120) and committing to completing the work involved. The Project Request Form asks for the signature of a parent or guardian to indicate that the family understands what the child is agreeing to do, and to enlist their participation.

Project Packets

Supervising teachers supply each student who has received permission to work on a specific project a Project Packet, a folder or envelope that includes the following:

- Approved Project Request Form
- Assignment Sheet and Assessment Form for the project selected
- Strategy Sheet
- List of Resources Form
- Project Log
- Midproject Report Form
- Program Evaluation Form
- Any other forms students might need for the specific project, such as group project checklists and Getting Started forms.

The packet ensures that students have all the forms and program information needed to begin working on a project. It can also be used to hold project materials. Supervising teachers should discuss the components of the packet when they hand it out to help students make sense of the process.

Strategy Sheet

The first step students need to take after receiving their Project Packet is to complete a Strategy Sheet (see pages 127–128). The Strategy Sheet asks students to develop a plan for completing and presenting their project. It asks them to define their specific topic and

think critically about all the steps involved, the materials they will need to gather, the research efforts they will invest, and the presentation or performance they will choose to demonstrate their learning. It also helps them create a tentative schedule by setting a due date for the Midproject Report and the final presentation. Supervising teachers should offer feedback and guidance to students to help them come up with a workable plan. A completed Strategy Sheet gives a good indication of how committed a student is to working on a project.

The Project Request Form and Strategy Sheet form the equivalent of a student learning contract. The student agrees to do a given project in a specified way within a designated time frame while being held accountable to an agreed-upon set of requirements and performance standards. By setting their own goals, students develop a sense of ownership of their projects and see themselves as engaged learners capable of directing their own learning.

List of Resources Form

Because independent research is such an important aspect of these projects, it's important that students record what resources they used to complete their project (see form on pages 129–130). Where did students find information and how can someone locate that source again? Asking students to record their sources helps them develop the habit of giving credit to others, raises awareness of plagiarism, and serves as a record for easy reference. It can also help teachers see the strengths and weaknesses in a student's research skills: Does a student skillfully incorporate information from a variety of appropriate sources? rely too heavily on a particular source? miss obvious sources of helpful information? keep good, organized records? Be sure to emphasize the importance of this step.

Project Log

Completing a Project Log (see pages 131–132) allows students to track the time they spend on the project. Recording their learning time serves many purposes. Students can see the actual time they've invested so far, and this can help motivate them to see the project through. It also can serve as a reminder that they are not working steadily enough, or help them plan their schedules for specific parts of the project. This form, too, provides space for parents to verify that the student talked to them about the tasks listed and (to the best of the parent's knowledge) completed the tasks.

What Happens at the Midproject Report?

Students schedule a date for giving a Midproject Report (see pages 133–134) to the supervising teacher when they fill out their Strategy Sheets. The Midproject Report outlines what progress students have made and establishes an interim deadline to help prevent procrastination. It prompts students to reflect on their work in progress and make any necessary adjustments to their original plans. It also gives the teacher an opportunity to offer feedback when it can be most helpful and to clarify any questions a student might have about expectations and how the final project will be assessed.

How Are Projects Assessed?

Each project comes with its own detailed Assessment Form. (See page 32 for an example.) Students receive the Assessment Form with the Project Packet so they understand from the beginning what criteria will be used for assessment. Discuss this form with students as they are working on their Strategy Sheet and again at the Midproject Report to clarify the expectations behind the assessment criteria. (For more on expectations, see pages 19–20. You and your students may want to detail the expectations more thoroughly.)

The Assessment Form provides space for three kinds of feedback:

a) Self-assessment. The column for self-assessment gives the student an opportunity to assess his or her achievements in the same areas as the supervising teacher. This is an important piece of the final evaluation. The student's estimation of his or her own work should be taken into account and discussed.

b) Supervising teacher assessment. The supervising teacher uses the same form to make a final assessment.

c) Other assessment. Many students and teachers find it helpful if members of small groups or project teams offer assessment information to each other. Peer tutors or student mentors may also complete an assessment, or perhaps a teacher with special expertise or a parent has something to contribute.

Supervising teachers and students rate each item on the Assessment Form on a scale of 1 to 4:

1 Showed Little or No Evidence That Expectations Were Achieved.

2 Needs Time to Achieve Expectations. Indicates that the project is incomplete or of poor quality. Perhaps given time to learn skills, gather more appropriate resources, rework portions of the project, or practice a performance technique, the student may be able to achieve expectations.

3 Achieved Expectations. Indicates that the student's work meets the minimum standards for the criterion.

4 Exceeded Expectations. Indicates that the student's work is superior—meaning all of the requirements were met with the very highest level of quality, beyond the minimum expectations.

It is important to note that the Assessment Form is not a fully developed rubric. An assessment *rubric* includes carefully written standards of quality that clearly describe expectations for each item. The Expectations Form (see page 146) will help you—and your students—develop written expectations that provide unambiguous guidelines for assessment.

It's best to allow students another chance to present their projects if they fail to meet expectations on the first try. They will undoubtedly learn from what went well and what didn't go as planned, and a second opportunity to present their work can be invaluable to their learning.

In addition to the numerical rating, written comments outlining the project strengths are an extremely valuable addition to the assessment feedback. Describe what the student did well and what aspects of the project were most impressive. This is perhaps the most meaningful input teachers can offer students. They will remember your encouraging remarks long after the assessment itself has faded from memory. The Written Comments form (see page 144) can be used to track a student's progress throughout the project. It will remind you of specific examples you can point to when writing a narrative evaluation.

Insert an assessment form into each student's permanent record folder to describe the project he or she completed.

How Do Students Get Credit for Their Work?

Students can receive credit for their work in a variety of ways, depending on how you set up the program within your school. The key is to set clear guidelines and recognize students who achieve their goals. Projects included in the regular classroom curriculum could be worked into an existing grading structure. Students who do a project as an extension or an enrichment opportunity should be given extra credit for their work. If the projects are offered as an independent study course or as

the basis for a gifted and talented program, students can earn a separate grade on their report cards. Some schools currently using the program require all students to complete a project for their graduation portfolio. Students put a tremendous amount of effort into completing projects, and it's important that they receive rewards commensurate to their efforts.

Small-Group Work

Many of these projects can be easily adapted to allow students to work in small groups. An experienced teacher who understands the dynamics of group work can help students modify a project to accommodate each student's strengths and interests. (Several forms are provided on pages 121–123 to help students get started.) Although group work requires the supervising teacher to assume additional responsibilities—helping to create a positive group climate and ensuring that team members develop the structure, organization, and assessment strategies needed for a successful project—the learning outcomes for students can be significant. And because group work mirrors the way many tasks are completed in the "real world," working on a team can enhance the authenticity of a project.

The projects work well for cooperative learning or other small-group structures, but the key to success is planning. Students involved in small-group projects don't always see the need for detailed planning. They can envision an ideal, spectacular outcome and can't wait to get started—especially if they have an opportunity to work with close friends. Partway through the project, however, problems may develop or the goal may start to seem vague or impossible to reach. Without a plan, students may lose confidence and want to quit. However, if they create, discuss, and agree upon a solid plan, students will have a realistic mental map of the process they can use to achieve their goal. Understanding the process gives them the power to develop strategies for solving problems that arise and, more important, provides the framework for group members to combine their best ideas.

Carefully structured group work can also offer a valuable opportunity for including struggling students in a creative and challenging project. Team experiences like Odyssey of the Mind and Science Olympiad illustrate how the synthesis of individual strengths can produce spectacular results. A student lacking the full repertoire of skills to complete a project on her own may excel in a group where her talents fill a specific need. This interdependent effort reflects how the real world operates. When it's successfully implemented in a school project, it can become the catalyst that sparks enthusiasm and renewed confidence in learning.

Group Assessment

When students decide to work in a group, make sure everyone understands from the beginning how the work will be assessed. You could set up one final assessment of the entire project with all group members receiving one project evaluation, but it's also important to assess each student's contribution. Students need to demonstrate how well they've met their own goals and what they've learned in the process. A group grade on a project intended to produce individual learning and creative expression can be unfair because it emphasizes the cooperative skills over learning. Assessment can be more complicated with groups, but the enriching effects on student learning can make it worthwhile.

Check It Out

Cooperation in the Classroom (6th edition) by David W. Johnson, Roger T. Johnson, and Edythe J. Holubec (Alexandria, Va.: ASCD, 1994). Based on years of research and experience with teachers, the authors guide educators in what to do before, during, and after cooperative learning lessons to maximize learning. A 14-part troubleshooting guide helps teachers monitor and help get groups back on track.

Groupwork in Diverse Classrooms: A Casebook for Educators edited by Judith H. Shulman, Rachel A. Lotan, and Jennifer A. Whitcomb (New York: Teachers College Press, 1998). Introduces readers to working with groups in diverse classrooms.

Maximizing Student Success

Many factors determine whether students will be successful in completing their projects and meeting the challenges involved. You can help increase students' success by making sure that they have the basic skills to do the project they've planned, by helping them create a workable plan, and by assuring clear expectations.

Basics for Success

Students need to have the fundamental skills, knowledge, and proficiencies they will be expected to apply during the project. Discuss the requirements for the project with students so that they understand the work involved and so that you both know what students will be learning along the way and what you may need to preteach. (See page 18 for more on determining the basics for success.)

Following a Workable Plan

Another way to ensure that students succeed is to help them come up with a workable plan on the Strategy Sheet and then review that plan and their progress on the Midproject Report. Planning is a very important part of the learning process, so be careful not to plan the project for students or, in your enthusiasm, inadvertently squelch their ideas with your own.

It's also common for students to think that when they run into difficulties, the project isn't working. Quite the opposite is true, however. Difficulties are a natural part of any project; problems give students opportunities to develop confidence as they think critically to find solutions. Difficulties also force students to be more creative, flexible, determined, and, consequently, more proud of their final projects. If supervising teachers view problems as a natural part of the process, they will give guidance that encourages students to meet the challenges that arise.

Maintaining Commitments

Some students, for one reason or another, may want to back out of their commitment to the project. Perhaps students working in a group have major disagreements on how to proceed and one or more members want to drop out. Perhaps a project eats up more time than expected. When these kinds of things happen, here are some steps you can take:

● From the beginning, counsel students to understand that in requesting a project they are entering into a contract. Develop procedures for letting students drop out of the program, but also clearly define consequences for not following through (for example, losing the right to start another project, or writing personal letters of explanation to everyone who will be affected by someone's decision to quit).

● Some students may want to quit because they have run into problems and don't have any strategies for working through them. Allowing students to back out at this point tells them that they aren't capable of succeeding. Establishing your belief in their ability to continue and giving them the support they need to solve problems helps them look at the project from another perspective and allows them to retain their dignity as they get back to work. Wanting to quit is a low point for students, but it's also an opportunity to restore confidence and help them achieve their dreams.

Other Ways to Encourage Success

Here are a few more ideas to maximize success:

● Students benefit from seeing examples of completed projects that others have done in previous years. Concrete examples show students the high quality of work their classmates have achieved, inspire ideas for new projects, and spark a spirit of friendly competition.

● Enlist parent participation from the beginning, and use their influence to help motivate students to complete the project on time.

● Concentrate efforts in two areas to help ensure that most students who participate complete their projects: (1) explain all expectations and procedures very clearly so that there are no surprises, and (2) make the program fun and inviting.

● Plan a big event (for example, an open house) where students can have fun showing off their finished projects. Take photos of students with their certificates, write an article for the newspaper about their achievements, or find other ways to celebrate the students' accomplishments.

● Because a public final presentation is built into each project, not finishing, or failing to achieve expected quality standards, will affect the public demonstration. The performance adds greater weight to the need to finish the project on time and with quality.

Final Presentations

Early in the planning you should discuss specific ways students can present their final projects to other people. Each student decides on a form of presentation at the planning stage of the project. This is an important decision, because the type of presentation a student chooses helps determine how to conduct the project. Students usually choose presentation styles that are most comfortable for them and that let them display their strongest areas of intelligence. The numerous possibilities for presentations include:

- oral presentation to the class or team teachers

- public display in the school building (posters, bulletin boards, models, diorama, exhibits, demonstrations, etc.)

- display in another public building (library, central administration office, nature center, museum, government offices, etc.)

- video presentation in the school or another public building

- written report, story, or poem with illustrations, for display in the media center or in elementary buildings for others to read

- article submitted to a newspaper or to a local television station

- lesson to younger children at an elementary school

- computer presentation, Web site, or software

- dramatic, musical, or artistic performance

- speech to an audience (student assembly, staff meeting, community group, etc.)

- special display during parent conference time

No matter how students choose to make their final presentation, supervising teachers should remind them to practice and offer guidance and support in making the arrangements for the presentation.

Certificates

Present certificates to students who have earned them. *Challenging Projects for Creative Minds* includes two kinds of certificates: a Certificate of Completion for students who meet project expectations and a Certificate of Merit for students who produce exceptional results (see pages 147–148). Supervising teachers, along with specialists who may be involved in certain projects, determine which certificate students will receive. Schools may want to use the reproducible certificates or design their own with the school's logo or motto. Either way, reproduce the certificates on high-quality paper to make them appealing and get original signatures from school officials. Consider inviting parents to a recognition luncheon, breakfast, or ceremony to present the certificates. An open house where the public can come to view finished projects is also an effective way to showcase student achievement and award certificates.

Evaluating the Program

Ask students and their parents to complete a program evaluation after students have completed a project. This is an important aspect of the program: Both students and parents should have a way to voice their opinions about the quality and value of the projects, and they need a formal method of offering suggestions for changes and improvements in the program. The Program Evaluation Form (see pages 137–138) provides a mechanism to collect comments, impressions, and ideas.

Sample Program

This section outlines one way schools can set up and conduct a schoolwide enrichment program using these materials. Many schools offer the program at the beginning of the school year, with students signing up for projects in the fall, working on them over the winter, and presenting their final projects in the spring. The concept is flexible, however, so every school can set up a program that fits its needs. Keep in mind that the first year of the program is usually a learning process for the staff and students as they discover what works best in their school.

Preprogram Planning

1. Hold a staff meeting to present the program and to discuss how it should be implemented. Allow teachers to look over the projects, and tentatively decide who the supervising teachers will be.

2. If necessary, hold another staff meeting to discuss program specifics:

- How will it be offered in the school?
- Who will organize and manage the program?
- Who will be the supervising teachers?
- When and how will the program be presented to students and their families?
- How will students be recognized at the end of the year?

3. Keep several copies of *Challenging Projects for Creative Minds* and the Project Request Forms on file in a central location, such as the media center, and determine who will be responsible for maintaining them.

4. Meet with supervising teachers to finalize how to present the program to students, how students will sign up, and when students can meet with their supervising teachers to discuss chosen projects.

Introducing the Program

1. Hold a meeting for students to introduce the program to them. Include:

- Program overview
- Project titles and descriptions
- Final presentations and certificates
- Sign-up procedures
- Which teachers are part of the supervising team (and can be contacted if there are questions during the sign-up process)
- Due date for Project Request Forms

2. Prominently display *Challenging Projects for Creative Minds* and the Project Request forms.

3. Collect Project Request Forms on the due date and meet to make a list of students who will participate in the program.

4. Notify students of their acceptance into the program:

- Inform students that their projects have been approved.
- Give each student the name of his or her supervising teacher.
- Ask students to contact their supervising teacher to set up a meeting to get their Project Packets and discuss their project plans.

5. Put Project Packets together for each student (see page 8).

6. Students meet with supervising teachers to receive Project Packets and to begin working on Strategy Sheets.

7. Students turn in finished Strategy Sheets and meet with supervising teachers to finalize plans.

8. Students begin working on projects.

Working the Program

1. Students meet with their supervising teachers to discuss how things are going.

2. Supervising teachers meet as a group to discuss the program so far and to determine if any adjustments need to be made in the process.

3. Students meet with their supervising teachers to go over the Midproject Report.

4. Supervising teachers check in with students to confirm that projects are nearly complete.

Presenting Projects

1. Students submit finished projects.

2. Students present their projects to supervising teachers.

3. Students complete their self-assessment.

4. Supervising teachers assess the projects.

5. The school holds a recognition event to showcase student achievement.

6. Students display or present their work publicly. (This can also be done at the student recognition event.)

How to Write a Project

Because every school's curriculum is different, educators may want to develop their own ideas into projects that meet specific school goals. Detailed instructions and forms will guide you in doing just that. They help you not only build your own projects, but clarify your learning goals and expectations for your students. Students who choose to do "Design Your Own Project" (see pages 112–116) may also use these forms to develop projects tailored to their interests and goals.

The first four forms guide you step by step in creating a ready-to-use project. The last two forms will help you articulate the standards for assessment and determine if students are ready to work on a project.

- Outcomes
- Introduction and Scenario
- Assignment
- Basics for Success
- Assessment Form
- Expectations (Standards for Assessment)

Outcomes

When developing a project, focus first on the results that you want. How will the project help students achieve important educational goals? In other words, try to answer the questions "Why are we doing this?" and "What results are we looking for?"

Before you begin creating the introduction and scenario, determine the outcomes you want students to achieve (see Outcomes Form on page 140). What will students accomplish by completing the project? You can base a project on outcomes established by your school district or goals you have for your students. A project may have many valuable outcomes, but to keep the system simple and easy to use, don't record more than four outcomes. Focusing on the three or four most important outcomes automatically defines the critical features of the project. Once you've determined the learning goals, you can move on to writing and shaping the project.

Introduction and Scenario

Everyone likes to do engaging projects, so the introduction and scenario can be designed to present a fun or interesting idea that appeals to students. The introduction gives an overview of the project and briefly explains what students will do. And the scenario provides an essential component of learning: a concrete *context* that makes sense to students and allows them to visualize doing the work. The scenario establishes a reason for learning specific content and skills. Once you've written the scenario, you can develop an assignment that includes activities and practice that will help your students meet the learning goals.

Guiding students to apply skills and content in authentic situations is exponentially more meaningful than simply teaching skills and content in isolation. You can find many ways to build the educational goals for your grade into a creative assignment. For example, let's say the scenario is that the student lives in the year 2199 and travels in a time machine to learn about life at the dawn of the twenty-first century. Students may be more eager to carry out the assignment tasks—study current events, conduct research, produce well-written paragraphs, design a poster, make an oral presentation, conduct an interview, etc.—because the scenario gives them a concrete reason to do so. And, of course, the ultimate payoff is that scenarios can help make learning fun. Students are quick to take advantage of the opportunity to personalize their projects. Tapping into student motivation is a key element in the success of Creative Minds projects.

When writing a scenario, describe a specific role that will help students visualize the task and make connections to familiar situations. Be sure to include what students will produce and how they will be expected to present their final project. Refer to projects in this book as examples.

Creating the Introduction and Scenario

You'll find a reproducible form for writing the Introduction and Scenario on page 141 to prompt you through the process:

Title: Think of a catchy title that hints at what the project is about.

Introduction: What does the project allow students to do? Why would students want to do this project? What could students gain from doing this project? How might it connect to students' lives?

Project Scenario:

- *Role.* What role will students play as they work on the project?

- *Assignment.* What will the students' tasks be in this role?

- *Products.* What tangible products will students create or develop?

- *Demonstration.* How will students demonstrate or present their work?

Assignment

As you develop the steps of the assignment that students will follow, build in the required skills, content, and processes established for your grade level. For example, if you write a project scenario in which the student heads a consumers-rights group that publishes the results of product testing, you might incorporate your school's graphing requirement—one of the assignment steps could require students to test various products and produce charts and graphs that compare product performance or quality.

Another goal in developing projects is to build in ways for students to make choices throughout the assignment so that they can use their strongest intelligences and work within their preferred learning styles. Giving students control to choose subject matter that interests them and to demonstrate their learning in ways that feel comfortable helps them learn to be more self-directed. Because students all work from different interests and connect their learning to different prior knowledge and different skills, the same project completed by thirty students will result in thirty unique finished projects. Your students will become motivated to learn because in addition to the structure that they need to achieve results, they will have the freedom to personalize and define the project as something they find relevant.

Develop the assignment by writing project requirements in a logical order of progression. (See the Assignment Form on page 142.) What must students do to successfully complete the project? Describe each component of the project as an assignment step. As you work on your draft, remember that the assignment should make sense within the context of the scenario that you've written. Renumber the steps if you change their order.

Outcomes Check

After you've written the requirements for the project on the Assignment Form, you'll want to review each step to make sure it helps students achieve one or more outcomes. Check your assignment against your desired outcomes. Every step should contribute directly to at least one learner outcome. If part of the assignment doesn't contribute to learner outcomes, reevaluate its purpose in the project. Similarly, every learner outcome should be included in the assignment. If an outcome isn't addressed in the assignment, you'll need to revise either your assignment or your expected outcomes. Aligning the assignment with outcomes strengthens the project and gives it educational validity.

Basics for Success

How do you know that a student is prepared to do a project? Often students don't perform as well as expected on assignments because they don't have the fundamental skills or knowledge necessary to succeed. For example, perhaps a student didn't locate enough information about a topic not because of laziness or lack of intelligence, but because he didn't know how to use available Internet resources. To succeed, students have to have the skills, knowledge, and proficiencies they will be expected to apply during the project.

As you develop your project, ask yourself, What background, skills, and proficiencies do students need to do this project? After listing these on the Basics for Success Form (see page 145), look at each basic skill or proficiency critically. For each one, ask yourself three questions:

1. Is it reasonable to expect students to apply this skill?

2. Have students mastered the skill?

3. Will preteaching or modeling be necessary before the project begins?

Based on your answers to these questions, you can determine the specific skills or knowledge necessary to prepare students for this project. The more preteaching and modeling required, the more time the project will take.

Example: Basic skills or knowledge students will need to do the project "Moments in Time":

1. Background knowledge about the historical period being studied.

2. Math skills to calculate a scale for the time line.

3. Measurement and drawing skills to properly lay out the time line.

4. Research skills for locating information about the topic.

5. Note-taking skills for recording information in an orderly way.

6. Basic writing skills (complete sentences and well-developed paragraphs).

7. Graphic art skills to produce a visually appealing display.

8. Critical-thinking skills to recognize important events.

9. Oral communication skills to explain the time line.

Assessment Form

The assessment criteria are an essential part of any worthwhile project for several reasons. Knowing what they will be assessed on shows students what will be expected of them *as they begin their projects,* so that they can successfully fulfill project requirements. The Assessment Form for each project clearly identifies what content students will learn, what artifacts they will produce, what processes they will use to complete the project, and how they will demonstrate that they've achieved the learner outcomes you've identified. A completed assessment form can become a permanent record of academic achievement that students can include in a portfolio.

The Assessment Form (see page 143) provides space for you to list the specific skills or tasks that each student will perform in completing the project. Refer to your Assignment Form as you develop the assessment items to be sure they correlate to what students were asked to do. Begin each item in the assessment with an active verb in the past tense (since students should have completed these requirements by the time they are assessed).

The Assessment Form has four sections:

1. Student Responsibilities. This section summarizes the main requirements of the project.

2. Process. This section lists the assignment steps that involve processes. *For example:* conducted an interview, applied research skills to find information, identified three sources of information about a sport, read a challenging book, developed a plan, solved problems independently, completed tasks on time.

Process tasks involve skills that translate to other areas of learning, regardless of subject area. Process skills are the basis for learning "how to learn." A person who is skilled at identifying problems and brainstorming ways to solve them, for example, can apply these skills to any situation, both now or in the future. Such skills aren't easily taught. They are best learned through projects that motivate students to take responsibility for their own learning: projects that give them choice, a context for learning, and a mandate to demonstrate their achievements to an audience. Process tasks must be attached to something tangible, a context or scenario that makes sense to the student. Process tasks acquire purpose when they are tied to the development of a product or artifact. The artifact becomes evidence that the student has applied learning to achieve something worthwhile.

3. Products. In this section, itemize what students produce during the project. *For example:* a journal, a brochure, a garden, a map.

4. Content. Record specific knowledge and concepts that students should have learned or applied while completing the project.

Remember, the Assessment Form is not a fully developed rubric. Some teachers write standards of quality that clearly describe expectations for each item. The Expectations Form (see page 146) will help you—and your students—develop written expectations that provide unambiguous guidelines for assessment.

Expectations

Students have better success when they fully understand the expectations of quality they are striving to achieve. Each project in this book includes an assessment form to guide in evaluating a student's project. Supervising teachers and students are both asked to assess how well the student met the expectations for the project, so understanding the expectations behind each assessment item is important.

The Assessment Forms for *Challenging Projects* do not include detailed assessment criteria because expectations vary from classroom to classroom. Expectations for a sixth grade student, for example, would be different than those for a tenth grader, and teachers working with special education students might have different criteria than teachers of gifted and talented students.

When you assess a student's finished project, you naturally have a certain set of expectations about what is satisfactory and what falls short for each item on the Assessment

Form. Some students exceed your expectations and receive a 4 rating, others do not. This set of expectations probably exists in your head and isn't available for students to reference. The Expectations Form (see page 146) will help you clarify what constitutes average achievement for each item on the assessment form. Writing out detailed assessment criteria for projects that you offer your students isn't mandatory; but it will establish your benchmarks for successful completion.

Some teachers hold a class discussion to establish assessment expectations. This gives students input on the criteria used to identify quality and encourages their ownership of final evaluations. Some items will require more detailed explanation than others. Regardless of whether you use the Expectations Form for projects that you create, or for existing projects from the book, in spelling out the expectations, you will improve the chances of a fair and consistent assessment for every student who completes a project, as well as the student's chances of success. Not everyone will have the time or the need to write out the expectations. But if you're trying to make consistent judgments about many projects, or if several teachers are assessing the projects, the Expectations Form can be a valuable tool for standardizing assessments.

Sample Expectations: Moments in Time

Requirement: Present 20 noted events.
Expectation: The student will record 20 historically correct noted events on the time line. The student will describe all noted events clearly and concisely, in one or two complete sentences. Each noted event is relevant to the topic and assigned to the correct time or date on the time line. No important events are omitted.

Requirement: Present six expanded events.

Expectation: The student will record six historically correct expanded events on the time line. The student will describe all six expanded events clearly in one or more properly developed paragraphs. All expanded events are relevant to the topic, thoughtfully chosen, and assigned the correct specific time or date on the time line.

Requirement: Present three focused events.
Expectation: The student will record three historically correct focused events on the time line. The student will choose focused events that are important or interesting, relevant to the topic, assigned to the correct time or date on the time line. The student will describe each focused event in detail, including at least one illustration that demonstrates the student's best visual presentation skills, as well as an engaging description written in two or more properly developed paragraphs.

Requirement: Present one primary event.
Expectation: The student will select one historically correct primary event—the most critical, important, or interesting event on the time line. The student's selection, which must be relevant to the topic and assigned to the correct time or date, is described in detail and includes at least two illustrations that demonstrate the student's best visual presentation skills, as well as a description written in three or more properly developed paragraphs. The student can provide oral justification for choosing the primary event.

Student Projects

Student Introduction

Have you ever had an idea that you wanted to explore, something you've wanted to learn, only to find it wasn't covered in class? Well, here's a chance to take charge of what you study and meet your own goals. *Challenging Projects for Creative Minds* lets you direct your own learning—

you get to choose a topic or project that you find interesting and worthwhile. These projects, which you can do on your own or in a small group, offer specific guidelines for completing the requirements, yet you have the freedom to decide what to study, what resources to use, and the best way to present your completed project.

Working on a project lets you develop skills that you'll use far beyond this year; you'll develop organization and planning skills, problem-solving techniques, self-discipline, self-assessment, and creativity to produce something that is uniquely yours. These skills apply to all areas of learning, and a great way to develop them is by working on in-depth projects.

But by making a plan and following it to complete a project, you'll gain more than these skills and knowledge about the topic you choose. You'll also gain tremendous confidence in yourself and your abilities because you've set a goal for yourself and acted on it. You demonstrate independence, gain a sense of accomplishment, and learn that you can make things happen in your life.

How Do These Projects Work?

Looking over the projects in the book, you'll notice that while they cover a wide variety of topic areas, they are all set up the same way.

Each one starts with an introduction and a scenario. The introduction talks about the subject of the project, and the scenario describes what you are being asked to do, why it needs to be done, and what you will produce. Assignment pages outline the project requirements and guide you in making choices to determine what form your final, completed project will take. The Assessment Form included with each project offers a checklist of what will be assessed after you turn in your work. It includes not only space for a teacher's feedback, but also a place for you to assess what you've accomplished.

While these projects are designed to be both educational and fun, the *Challenging Projects for Creative Minds* program requires a commitment from you to complete the work once your project is approved. Once you sign on, you will be expected to follow through. Keep in mind that while you'll be in charge of your own learning and direct your own work, you'll also have the support and guidance of a supervising teacher throughout the project. If you have problems or questions you can't resolve, your supervising teacher can help you come up with solutions or learn a new skill. You will be encouraged to consult additional school staff or other adults who have knowledge in your topic area or could help in other ways—for example, by recommending resources, giving technological assistance, teaching skills you may need to do your project, providing insight and encouragement, and helping you arrange your final performance or display.

Part of the planning you'll do to organize your project includes deciding early on how to present your final work to others. (You might want to check out the list on page 115 for ideas.) After you've presented your final project to your supervising teacher, you will also present it publicly in some manner, either at school or in your community. Depending on your topic, you might arrange to display your work at elementary schools, libraries, community groups, art museums, nature centers, or other public locations.

Finally, you'll be awarded a certificate in recognition of your success. Students who present a finished project will be awarded a Certificate of Completion; those who demonstrate work of exceptional quality will receive a Certificate of Merit.

The goal of the program is to offer each student who accepts the challenge an opportunity to show what he or she can do. We all have heroes and role models, but we don't admire these people because of their test scores or the grades they receive in school. Rather, we admire them for their accomplishments, for what they give the world. These projects are designed to let you demonstrate what you can achieve, to produce something not just for a teacher to grade but to share with others.

Everyone has strengths and abilities. Do you know what yours are? Have you considered what you will do with them or how important they may be for your future? Consider doing a project to find out. You have a choice.

Here is the process for completing a project:

1. Examine the project choices closely. Think about your interests and goals and discuss the projects with a supervising teacher. Read the projects carefully and talk about them with friends or at home with your family. Choose the project that best fits your interests and learning goals.

2. Once you decide that you do want to complete a project, fill out a Project Request Form (see page 120), get a parent or guardian's signature, and turn it in for approval.

3. Upon receiving approval, schedule a meeting with your supervising teacher to discuss your plans.

4. Go over the Project Packet with your supervising teacher. This packet contains:

- Your approved Project Request Form

- Project Assignment Sheets and Assessment Form

- Strategy Sheet

- List of Resources Form

- Project Log

- Midproject Report Form

- Program Evaluation Form

- Any other forms, such as group project forms, that you might need

5. Outline your plan for completing the project on a Strategy Sheet (see pages 127–128). You'll be asked to think through your project and organize the steps you'll take in completing it. You'll set up a schedule, list the materials you'll need, and decide how you'll present your project.

6. Review your plan with your supervising teacher.

7. Begin working on your project. Every project requires some research. Record the resources you use on the List of Resources (see pages 129–130). List all your sources so that you can find them again if you need them and include them in your list of works cited for your final project.

8. Keep track of the time you spend and the tasks you complete on a Project Log (see pages 131–132). The Project Log not only documents your progress, but it also helps remind you to keep moving the project toward completion. Reviewing what you've already done will help you determine what areas may need more time and effort. It will show your supervising teacher how your plan is progressing and serve as a reference for your self-assessment.

9. Meet regularly with your supervising teacher for support and guidance. Be sure to ask questions as they arise.

10. Complete a Midproject Report Form (see pages 133–134) to show what progress you've made. This is a chance to reflect on how the project is going and make any needed changes to your plan. Meet with your teacher to discuss the project: What's going well? Have you encountered any unexpected problems? Have you discovered exciting and new information? Does your time line still seem workable? Do you need to change aspects of your plan?

11. Continue to work steadily to complete the project.

12. Once you complete your project, present it to your supervising teacher.

13. Fill out the self-assessment section on the Assessment Form (for an example, see page 32).

14. Discuss the project assessment with your supervising teacher.

15. Turn in a Program Evaluation Form, including your parent's or guardian's signature (see pages 137–138).

16. Accept your Certificate of Merit or Certificate of Completion.

17. Present your project publicly.

Working in Groups

Many students prefer to work together, and that option can help you succeed with these projects—provided you're willing to put in extra planning time up front. The requirements for group work are the same as those for individuals, but you have greatly expanded the possibilities for your final presentations.

Groups can accomplish much more than people working in isolation.

If you decide to work in a group, you need to plan how you'll do this. Group members might choose to work on individual products, offering each other support and feedback and integrating their work into a cohesive final group presentation. For example, to create an art exhibit for the project "Express Yourself" (see pages 45–49), you and other group members might decide on a theme for the exhibit and then each create your own works of art. For your final presentation, you'd display your work together in a comprehensive exhibit. Each person would be responsible for an individual display and be assessed on all items on the evaluation.

Or you might decide to divide project responsibilities based on your individual strengths and interests. For example, if you decide to put together a magazine for the project "The Desktop Publisher" (see pages 86–91), you could divide responsibilities much as a professional publisher might: One person is primarily responsible for the writing; another for the cover, layout, and illustrations; and another for project management and the technical skills of putting it all together on the computer. Working as a team allows group members to combine complementary strengths and abilities to produce a truly dynamic final project.

To work on a project as a group, first make sure that all members are serious about combining efforts, that you have firmly established goals and assigned roles that everyone understands, and that each person has the maturity to contribute to a team effort. You may be asked to complete a detailed series of planning forms (see pages 121–123) to make sure that everyone understands what the project entails.

Tips for Working in a Group

1. You don't have to be close friends to work well together.

2. Respect each other's opinions and listen to each other's ideas. And respect your own opinions—be sure to offer your ideas as well.

3. Each group member has something to contribute. Because no one is good at everything, working as a group lets you take advantage of everyone's special strengths, whether they're in leadership, organization, planning, brainstorming, mathematics, mediation, artistry, music, writing, speaking, drama, logical thinking, humor, optimism, confidence, risk-taking, common sense, creativity, technological savvy . . . you get the idea.

4. During a project, you'll inevitably run into problems that need to be solved, conflicts that need resolution, things that just don't go right. By working together to deal with each situation, your group will think of new ideas to improve your project and make it stronger. Don't be discouraged by setbacks. They offer you the opportunity to do better.

5. Encourage each other and support each other's efforts. The smallest things can make a difference. Listen to each other, share stories about yourselves, think critically but don't criticize, don't take constructive suggestions personally, laugh together, and point out what you like about the work as you go along.

6. Use your imagination. The project requirements may sound specific, but every assignment asks you to make choices and think of creative ways to design your final presentation. Group brainstorming sessions can produce some very effective results as one person's idea gives someone else another great idea. After a few minutes of "Hey, I know!" or "I've got an idea!" or "Listen to this . . ." you'll exclaim, "Let's do that!"

7. Don't forget the details. The extra effort that you put into making things interesting will not go unnoticed.

Project Choices

 Menagerie from the Mind—Zoology

Map an imaginary island and invent animals to inhabit it. The project involves classifying animals, designing a food web, describing adaptations, and illustrating body systems.

 It's Written in the Stars—Astronomy

Design an exhibit for a science museum to introduce people to a fascinating topic in astronomy.

 Moments in Time—History

Choose a topic that interests you, design a time line that presents events in order, and focus on several of the most critical events.

 And Now for the News—Current Events

Choose a current events topic and create a storyboard to show how it might be presented as a television program for middle school students.

 Express Yourself—Art

Create an exhibit of your original art, and produce a brochure that gives information about the exhibit.

 Media Master—Multimedia

Use your computer skills to develop a simple multimedia program about a topic of your choice.

 Honored Athlete—Sports Statistics

Analyze the performance of veteran athletes by examining their performance statistics over a five-year period.

 Time of My Life—Survey Analysis

Design and conduct a poll to find out how much time students your age devote to everyday activities. Organize and analyze your data, and display the results of your work.

 In Other Words—Languages

Create a new product in a language other than English. You don't need to be fluent in a foreign language to participate.

 Great Performances—Performing Arts

Plan a public performance of your talents—whether dance, music, drama, or juggling—and present it to an audience.

Local Hero—Journalism

Interview a "local hero" (someone in the community whom you respect and admire) and produce an article that could be published in a newspaper.

Now Presenting—Conference Planning

Organize a mini-conference for students in your school. Choose an interesting and timely topic to get students thinking.

The Time Traveler—Popular Culture

Cast yourself in the role of a time traveler from the future and visit the dawn of the twenty-first century to study the life and times of an ancestor.

The Desktop Publisher—Magazine Publishing

Create a magazine for people your own age. Use computers to design, lay out, and produce one issue of the magazine.

Sports Specialist—Athletic Training

Choose a sport and design a training program that athletes could follow to improve their performance.

Let Me Illustrate—Book Design and Illustration

Read a challenging book, illustrate several scenes from the story, and choose one to use on a jacket for a new edition of the book.

What's My Line?—Career Exploration

Choose a career to explore, research the career, and develop a map to show possible paths to that job.

May I Help You?—Service Learning

Become involved in your community with a service-learning project. Choose a local cause you are interested in, and create and follow a plan for personal involvement.

Student Mentor—Mentorship

Become an assistant, helping other students as they work on *Challenging Projects for Creative Minds*.

Design Your Own Project

Is there another topic that you would like to study? Students who have already completed at least one project can develop their own project from scratch.

From *Challenging Projects for Creative Minds* by Phil Schlemmer, M.Ed., and Dori Schlemmer © 1999. Free Spirit Publishing Inc., Minneapolis, MN; 800/735-7323; *www.freespirit.com*. This page may be photocopied for individual, classroom, or group work only.

Menagerie from the Mind

Zoology

In centuries past, naturalists such as Carolus Linnaeus, Charles Darwin, and Mary Anning scoured the planet studying new fossils, plants, and animals. Even today, biologists and archeologists are discovering plants and animals that were previously unknown. More than a million known species of animals roam the globe, and many more have yet to be discovered. Plants and animals adapt to their environment in incredible ways—from the chameleon that changes color to blend in with its background to the platypus with its duck bill and webbed feet for moving through the water. The diversity of life continues to capture the imagination of scientists around the world.

This project gives you an opportunity most scientists only dream of: to discover a previously unknown island inhabited by animals no person has ever seen before. Your task is to apply what you know about real animals to create animals that exist only in your imagination. You will invent a group of animals and classify them by describing their adaptations, body systems, predator-prey relationships, habitats, and other characteristics. The animals you invent must be realistic enough to live in habitats found on Earth. (In other words, this is not an opportunity to create animals with titanium shields and laser eyes and bombs packed under their wings.) The animals you "discover" can be unusual, even bizarre, but you must fit them into a real animal *taxonomy,* or classification system, and they must have characteristics that could occur in the natural world. This project lets you use your imagination to demonstrate your understanding of nature and animals.

Project Scenario

You are a naturalist who has discovered a small, previously unknown island that has been isolated from the rest of the world for millennia. Animals that no human has seen before inhabit the island. The National Zoo in Washington, D.C., has asked you to develop an exhibit describing your discoveries to zoo visitors. You have complete creative control to design the exhibit, but it must capture the interest of visitors and teach them about the animals and the island.

Assignment

Your exhibit may take many forms. It is up to you to decide how to fulfill the requirements of the project, which are listed below:

1. Describe the climate of the island you discover. It can be in arctic, temperate, or tropical waters. Use a world map to pinpoint the island's location in one of the oceans, far from the nearest known land. Give the island's longitude and latitude coordinates.

2. Make a map of the island. Be as detailed as possible and show all of the habitats that are available for animal life.

3. Invent at least eight animals and make sketches of them. Give each animal both a common name and a two-word scientific name designating its genus and species. For example, humans are *Homo sapiens*. Classify each animal and explain the characteristics that put the animal into its *taxa*, or classification groups. You must invent at least one animal from each of these classes: insect, fish, amphibian, reptile, bird, mammal.

How Do Scientists Classify Plants and Animals?

Taxonomy is the science of naming plants and animals in a way that reflects their natural relationships. Carolus Linnaeus, a Swedish botanist in the eighteenth century, developed a system called *binomial nomenclature* that's still in use today. In this system, each living thing has a two-part Latin name describing its genus and species. *Homo sapiens*, for example, is the name for human beings. The table below describes the other taxonomic levels for humans:

Taxonomic Level	Name	Distinguishing Feature
Kingdom	Animalia	animal
Phylum	Chordata	spinal cord
Class	Mammalia	young are breast-fed
Order	Primates	most highly developed
Family	Hominidae	two-legged
Genus	Homo	human
Species	sapiens	modern human

Provide the following information for each animal you discover:

- Identify each animal as a carnivore (meat-eater), an omnivore (eater of both animals and plants), or a herbivore (plant-eater). Only one of the animals should be a top predator (that means that nothing eats it). Of the remaining seven animals, identify two as intermediate predators, two as omnivores, and three as herbivores.

- Give each animal at least two items for its diet. Carnivores will eat two other animals on the island; herbivores will eat two plants that you invent; omnivores will eat one animal and one plant.

- Describe each animal's habitat with as much detail as possible.

- Describe at least two adaptations that each animal has developed to help it survive in its environment. Take the climate of your island into account.

4. Produce a food web that shows the relationships between the plants and animals on your island. In your web, connect each animal with the animals or plants that it eats by using arrows that point from the prey to the predator. Be prepared to answer questions about the food web.

5. Choose one of the animals and describe at least six adaptations in detail. Make drawings and written explanations to show how the animal is adapted to find and eat food, protect itself and its young, build homes, travel, communicate, blend into its surroundings, and so forth. Be prepared to answer questions about this animal and how it has adapted to the island.

6. Choose one of the animals and describe at least one of its body systems in detail. Through drawings and written explanations, illustrate one of these systems: digestive, respiratory, circulatory, sensory (seeing, hearing, etc.), central nervous, skeletal, or temperature regulating. Be as thorough as possible in your description, and be prepared to answer questions about the system you describe.

7. Write a short essay on what will happen to these animals and the island now that they have been discovered. Who will make the decisions? What specific measures, if any, should people take to protect them? What if people suggest putting the animals in zoos, or if travel companies plan to offer tours of the island, or if the nation that owns the island decides to develop it? Use real examples to support your points. Is it important to protect the island? Who will enforce your plan?

8. Combine all the elements of your project to create and present the exhibit you've planned.

Notes

_____

_____

_____

_____

_____

_____

_____

_____

_____

Menagerie from the Mind

GETTING STARTED

STUDENT NAME

Use this form to start thinking about your project. You will need to use a notebook or index cards to record detailed information as you invent and describe the details of each animal's habitat, diet, and adaptations.

Island's climate: _____

Island's location (include longitude and latitude): _____

Ideas for animals (choose eight): _____

_____

CLASS OF ANIMAL (bird, insect, etc.)	COMMON NAME	SCIENTIFIC NAME (genus/species)
1.		
2.		
3.		
4.		
5.		
6.		
7.		
8.		

CARNIVORE/OMNI-VORE/HERBIVORE	DIET (two items)	HABITAT	ADAPTATIONS (list two)
1.			
2.			
3.			
4.			
5.			
6.			
7.			
8.			

Menagerie from the Mind

ASSESSMENT FORM

STUDENT NAME

Student Responsibilities

- Create a map of an imaginary island, showing climate, habitats, and coordinates.
- Invent, draw, and classify at least eight animals; then describe two adaptations for each.
- Develop a complete food web for the animals, using arrows to show the relationships.
- Produce a detailed look at the adaptations (at least six) of one animal.
- Describe and illustrate how at least one body system functions in one of the animals.
- Compose an essay describing what's next for the animals and the island.
- Demonstrate knowledge of animals and ecosystems by answering reasonable questions from your supervising teacher and other exhibit-goers.
- Combine all elements into an exhibit and present it.

ASSESSMENT SCALE

4 Exceeded Expectations

3 Achieved Expectations

2 Needs Time to Achieve Expectations

1 Showed Little or No Evidence that Expectations were Achieved

	SELF	TEACHER	OTHER
PROCESS			
1. Selected the climate in which animals live.			
2. Demonstrated creative thinking skills.			
3. Applied research skills to find information and cited sources.			
4. Invented at least eight imaginary animals.			
5. Completed tasks in a timely manner.			
6. Solved problems independently.			
7. Applied writing skills to express ideas.			
8. Applied art skills to express ideas.			
9. Demonstrated a commitment to quality.			
10. Presented information effectively.			
PRODUCTS			
11. Created a detailed map and provided coordinates.			
12. Produced drawings of at least eight animals.			
13. Designed a detailed, graphic food web.			
14. Identified two adaptations for each animal.			
15. Illustrated six adaptations for one animal.			
16. Illustrated one body system for one animal.			
17. Composed an essay about what will happen to the animals.			
18. Combined materials to create an exhibit.			
19. Produced a well-organized exhibit.			
20.			
CONTENT			
21. Clearly defined and described habitats.			
22. Applied knowledge of animal classification.			
23. Demonstrated understanding of food webs.			
24. Applied knowledge of predators and prey.			
25. Analyzed an animal's adaptations.			
26. Analyzed an animal's body system.			
27. Gave informed answers to questions.			
28.			
29.			
30.			

It's Written in the Stars

Astronomy

People around the world and throughout the ages have watched and wondered about the stars and other celestial bodies. Over the centuries, their questions and observations have shaped the science of astronomy. With technological advances, scientists learn more and more about space and the universe and the physical properties of the natural world both on Earth and beyond. These discoveries have profoundly changed how people think about our planet, the solar system, and a mystifying universe.

This project offers you the opportunity to choose a topic in astronomy that interests you and study it in depth. Your job is to produce an exhibit that will teach others about the topic you've explored.

Project Scenario

You are a young scientist who has just graduated with a degree in astronomy, hoping to get a job at your local planetarium. The planetarium director had been looking for an assistant with several years of experience, but after reviewing your resume, she's decided to give you a shot at the new position. She has hired you on a temporary basis to develop an astronomy exhibit on a topic you choose and present it to the planetarium's board of directors. The board will ask you questions and judge your proposed exhibit on its appearance, completeness, accuracy, creative approach, and, above all, its educational value. Your task is to create an exhibit that will get you a permanent job at the planetarium.

Assignment

Your astronomy exhibit must meet specific guidelines, but you will decide on the topic, content, and organization. Here are the requirements:

1. Choose a topic. The field of astronomy offers an endless supply of fascinating topics. Take some time to explore the obvious—and not so obvious—possibilities before making a final decision. (See page 126 for help in narrowing down a topic.) Here's a brief list to help you get thinking about possibilities:

- measuring distances in space
- the Apollo space program
- the Big Bang theory
- the Hubble space telescope
- Earth's path through space
- astronomical time
- comets (Hale-Bopp, for example)
- sun spots and solar activity
- the surface of the moon
- how telescopes work
- how scientists study stars
- black holes
- life aboard a space station
- gravity
- the Mars Pathfinder Sojourner expedition
- asteroids

Check It Out

Astronomy (Teach Yourself) by Patrick Moore (Lincolnwood, IL: NTC, 1995) is a good beginning book on astronomy. It makes difficult concepts easier to understand and doesn't assume readers have prior knowledge of astronomy.

Windows to the Universe
www.windows.ucar.edu
This University of Michigan site offers information on just about everything astronomical. A great resource for middle and high school students.

2. Conduct research on your topic. Begin by developing your research questions. What information do you need to find? Because all information in your educational exhibit must be accurate, research is a vital part of the process.

As you collect information, think about the exhibit. How will each fact that you record contribute to the exhibit that you are beginning to design in your mind? Narrow your focus early so you can restrict your research to topics directly connected to the exhibit you are planning. When you find something useful, write it down. Record individual facts on index cards so you can easily organize your research later by simply rearranging the index cards on your desk. Also be prepared to let your ideas about the exhibit be influenced by information you find. You might run across a terrific resource that completely changes how you think about the exhibit. Keep an open mind about what the exhibit will look like and what it will contain until you've gathered most of your data and begun to plan how to present it.

3. Plan the exhibit. Think about what kinds of displays (posters, drawings, photographs, reports, diagrams, graphs, models, video, sound recording, and so forth) will best convey your information. Can you include any hands-on activities for museum visitors? List everything you intend to develop for the exhibit. Describe briefly what each component will look like and what it will teach, explain, or display. Make a sketch or diagram to show how the exhibit will look when it's complete.

Discuss the list and the exhibit drawing with your supervising teacher. If your teacher agrees that you have produced a good plan, you may begin working on the exhibit. Talk with your supervising teacher to help arrange the location and setup for your exhibit.

4. Create the exhibit. As you develop each artifact, keep your audience in mind. People will spend time at an exhibit that captures their attention and gives them interesting things to think about. Remember also that your reason for doing this is to get a job at the planetarium. The hiring decision depends on the quality of the exhibit: its appearance, completeness, accuracy, creative approach, and, above all, its educational value. Keep these aspects in mind as you develop the exhibit that you've planned.

5. Set up your exhibit; present it to the planetarium board—your supervising teacher and others.

Notes

_____

_____

_____

_____

_____

_____

_____

_____

_____

_____

_____

_____

_____

_____

_____

_____

_____

_____

_____

_____

It's Written in the Stars

ASSESSMENT FORM

STUDENT NAME

Student Responsibilities

- Choose an astronomy topic to study.
- Conduct research to locate and record information about the topic.
- Design an exhibit for displaying information about the topic.
- Produce materials to include in the exhibit that help explain the topic.
- Present an astronomy exhibit that will teach others.
- Demonstrate knowledge by answering reasonable questions about the topic.

ASSESSMENT SCALE

4 Exceeded Expectations

3 Achieved Expectations

2 Needs Time to Achieve Expectations

1 Showed Little or No Evidence that Expectations were Achieved

	SELF	TEACHER	OTHER
PROCESS			
1. Chose an acceptable astronomy topic.			
2. Applied research skills to find information and cited sources.			
3. Planned an astronomy exhibit.			
4. Applied writing skills to express ideas in words.			
5. Applied creative skills to express ideas visually.			
6. Demonstrated creative-thinking skills.			
7. Completed tasks in a timely manner.			
8. Solved problems independently.			
9. Demonstrated a commitment to quality.			
10. Presented information effectively.			
PRODUCTS			
11. Produced the following: (list on lines below)			
12.			
13.			
14.			
15.			
16.			
17.			
18.			
19.			
20.			
CONTENT			
21. Demonstrated knowledge of the topic.			
22. Offered clear, simple examples.			
23. Utilized diagrams, models, charts, posters, and objects where appropriate.			
24. Identified and explained important concepts.			
25. Presented accurate information.			
26. Answered questions about the topic.			
27.			
28.			
29.			
30.			

Moments in Time

History

One way to learn about history is to study a series of events closely in chronological order. When we examine events in sequence, we can better see patterns of cause and effect and trace the development of ideas over time. That helps us understand not only *what* happened but

why it happened. For example, if you've ever boarded an airplane and experienced the excitement of taking off and rising into the sky, you've lived the dream that drove the Wright brothers to invent a machine that could fly. How did we get from the dream of flight to the point where the Concorde can cross the Atlantic Ocean in less than four hours?

This project gives you an opportunity to look closely at an important topic by creating a time line. Whether your interest is science, music, sports, fashion, politics, art, or ancient civilizations, you will gain a fuller understanding of the topic you choose. You will select a significant event and examine the sequence of smaller events it encompasses,

analyzing how they contribute to the big picture, and interpreting the event for others. In this project, your job is to create a detailed time line of a topic that you find significant. Here are some examples of topics to get your thinking process started:

- the Battle of Gettysburg
- the history of jazz
- the story of the ancient Egyptians
- a space shuttle mission
- the presidency of John F. Kennedy
- the history of baseball
- an overview of twentieth century women's clothing
- the building of the New York City subway system
- the works of a favorite artist or author

Project Scenario

You are a scholar who has been hired to create a new museum exhibit. You decide to develop an illustrated time line that explains a topic from your area of expertise. This is a fantastic opportunity to educate museum visitors. Because of your reputation for creating accurate, visually appealing presentations, all of the decisions about the exhibit's design and focus have been left up to you. Your finished time line will be prominently displayed at the museum.

Assignment

Here are the requirements for your time line display:

1. Select a general topic area for your time line. Once you've come up with a strong possibility for a topic, develop research questions and scan resources to help refine your focus. Talk to a librarian to help locate resources if necessary. (See page 126 for help in narrowing your topic.)

2. Once you have some initial information about your topic, choose an appropriate time frame for the time line you'll create. In other words, decide at what point in time you will begin and when you will end your time line. The Battle of Gettysburg, for example, lasted three days; the presidency of John F. Kennedy lasted about three years.

3. Each entry you make on the time line is called an *event*. Identify at least thirty major or significant events that you can note on the time line. Describe these *noted events* briefly, in one or two sentences. A convenient way to do this is to write about each event on an index card. Be sure to record the correct timing of each event so that the information can be transferred accurately to your time line.

4. Use what you've learned about your topic to choose the ten most significant events of your thirty noted events and expand upon them. (This leaves twenty noted events to record on your time line in step 8.) Describe these *expanded events* in one or more paragraphs.

5. Choose four of the ten expanded events and focus on them in more detail. (This leaves six expanded events to be recorded on the time line in step 8.) These should be four of the most critical, important, or interesting events on the time line. Provide some kind of illustrations as well as a written description for each of these *focused events*. On the time line, a focused event could look like a poster.

6. Choose the focused event that you consider to be the most critical, important, or interesting event on the time line. (This leaves three focused events to record on the time line in step 8.) This is called the *primary event*. Give the primary event significant space on the time line to include all your information—illustrations and descriptive paragraphs. Be prepared to discuss the primary event orally, answer questions about it, and explain your reasons for selecting it.

7. Develop a scale to use on the time line. This requires some thought and calculation. For example, on a 20-foot time line the scale for the Battle of Gettysburg (which lasted three days) might be 1 inch = 20 minutes. For John F. Kennedy's presidency (which lasted three years), it could be 1 inch = 5 days. Put the scale across the top edge of the time line paper by making periodic marks and recording units of time.

8. Complete the time line by recording all thirty events on it. This includes:

- 20 noted events
- 6 expanded events
- 3 focused events with illustrations
- 1 primary event with illustrations

9. Display your finished time line and be prepared to answer questions.

Look at the example below to see what part of a finished time line might look like.

Check It Out

Today in History

lcweb2.loc.gov/ammem/today

Maintained by the Library of Congress, this site features a daily historical event, often supplemented with photos, manuscripts, recordings, or other documents available from the Library's collection. Visitors can search the site or browse an archive of past dates.

The History Channel

www.historychannel.com

The History Channel offers a wealth of resources on many topics. It also lets you search for any day of the year and pull up interesting happenings from that day, annotated with facts and occasional supplementary URLs or video clips.

Notes

_____

_____

_____

_____

_____

_____

_____

_____

_____

_____

_____

_____

_____

_____

Moments in Time

ASSESSMENT FORM

STUDENT NAME

Student Responsibilities

- Design a time line that describes a topic by presenting events in correct order.
- Demonstrate an understanding of selected events by writing explanations.
- Illustrate selected events to visually represent what happened.
- Explain the connections between the primary event and other events on the time line.
- Justify your selection of the primary event by explaining its significance in relation to the other events on the time line.
- Present a finished time line.
- Demonstrate knowledge of the primary event by answering reasonable questions.

ASSESSMENT SCALE

4 Exceeded Expectations

3 Achieved Expectations

2 Needs Time to Achieve Expectations

1 Showed Little or No Evidence that Expectations were Achieved

	SELF	TEACHER	OTHER
PROCESS			
1. Chose a valid topic that fits the criteria.			
2. Identified at least thirty events.			
3. Applied research skills to find information.			
4. Developed an accurate scale for the time line.			
5. Completed tasks in a timely manner.			
6. Solved problems independently.			
7. Applied writing skills to express ideas.			
8. Applied art skills to express ideas.			
9. Demonstrated a commitment to quality.			
10. Presented information effectively.			
PRODUCTS			
11. Exhibited original thinking (layout and design).			
12. Designed an informative time line display.			
13. Assigned each event to a correct position.			
14. Produced a well-organized time line.			
15. Presented twenty noted events.			
16. Presented six expanded events.			
17. Presented three focused events.			
18. Presented one primary event.			
19.			
20.			
CONTENT			
21. Selected relevant and significant events.			
22. Produced well-written explanations.			
23. Produced art illustrating specific events.			
24. Described the flow of events in the correct order.			
25. Showed understanding of the topic.			
26. Showed understanding of a primary event.			
27. Gave informed answers to questions.			
28.			
29.			
30.			

And Now for the News

Current Events

Television news magazines are perennial viewer favorites. The journalists who produce these shows report and interpret current events to keep people informed about what is happening in the nation and the world. *And Now for the News* focuses on current events in a similar way.

You have the opportunity to choose an event that interests you, study it in depth, and explain it to people your age.

Your main task is to plan and produce a storyboard for one segment of an imaginary television news show that targets students your age. (You don't actually need to produce the show, although you certainly may.)

This project provides an excellent opportunity to work with a partner or as part of a team, much like journalists do in real life. You may also work alone, if you prefer.

people ages ten to sixteen. The president of a major network has asked you to develop a proposal for a brand-new TV news magazine about the world and current events. The series is designed to introduce young people to current events, discuss current issues and trends, and explain why young people need to be informed. Your job is to choose a topic for a pilot episode and develop a storyboard to show how you would create a short segment for this new series. You will present your ideas to network officials for approval.

Project Scenario

You and your partner are television producers who specialize in programming for young

Assignment

You have creative control over the issue you decide to tackle and how you'll organize your television segment, but you must adhere to network guidelines in creating your storyboard proposal. Here are the requirements for this project:

1. Research the event or issue you choose to cover. Besides the library, what other resources are available? Does your school have a teacher who teaches about the media? What Internet sites focus on your topic? What organizations may have helpful information? Who can you interview? Where can you find experts on your topic? As you conduct research and accumulate information, make notes about topics that you want to include in your television program. How will you present them so that kids can understand? (Be sure to keep track of your sources of information. The form on pages 129–130 can help.)

2. Watch examples on TV to see how journalists structure their stories, or ask a librarian for help finding resources on newswriting. When you have a sense of how to present your information, develop an outline for your television segment that organizes your main topics into a logical order that will inform a viewer. Use subheadings under main topics to indicate important events that you will discuss. Make sure your outline answers the 5 Ws: who, what, when, where, why.

3. Think about how your story might look to viewers—what will the camera record as your news story unfolds? Record ideas for graphics or pictures that could be used to illustrate each topic or event. Also think about what viewers will hear while watching the segment. Will the narrator or interviewer be on screen or off screen? Will there be music, sound effects, or background noise? Add these details to your outline, making adjustment where needed.

Check It Out

How to Write a News Article by Michael Kronenwetter (New York: Franklin Watts, 1995). This book introduces the basics of news journalism, including judging what is newsworthy, gathering information, journalistic ethics and bias, and shaping a story.

The Write Site
www.writesite.org
This journalism site has a great range of resources for students, including Newsroom, which guides you through investigating, planning, and writing news stories.

---

4. Produce a first-draft storyboard that has at least twenty-five panels. An example is provided on page 43. A storyboard shows how you want each scene to look and describes what will be said at that moment. It gives you an idea of what the TV segment will look like from start to finish. You want to create a smooth and natural transition from one scene to the next. Think carefully about what your news story will show viewers for each part. Describe each visual scene, the text or narration, other background sounds, and any special effects you'd like to use, such as titles or arrows to help explain what's happening. Does your story flow smoothly?

5. Collect or produce a visual image for each panel of your storyboard. Provide a picture, drawing, photograph, or sketch for each graphic on your final storyboard. You may use pictures from magazines, newspapers, or other sources if you can find them. If you can't locate just the right image for a particular scene, you may need to adjust your text. What other choices could you make to show viewers what is happening? Do not permanently attach graphic images to your first draft efforts; you'll probably be moving things around.

6. Show the first draft to your supervising teacher for advice and suggestions. You might also show it to another adult for additional input (a subject-area expert, a teacher, a parent, or an adult friend).

7. Develop a final storyboard that is as complete and clear as you can possibly make it. A storyboard is usually displayed in a series of panels on a wall, but when your presentation is finished, you can bind your panels into a large book.

8. Present the final-draft storyboard to the network officials (your supervising teacher and an audience of other students or teachers). Use the storyboard to describe the program segment you have developed and present your news segment. Be sure to explain why your topic is newsworthy and why you think your audience will be interested. Be prepared to answer questions about your topic and storyboard.

Image on camera:

Description of scene: _____
_____
_____

Narration: _____
_____
_____
_____

Background sounds or music: _____
_____
_____

Special effects: _____
_____
_____

And Now for the News

ASSESSMENT FORM

STUDENT NAME

Student Responsibilities

- Study a current event or issue, focusing on its importance to young people.
- Develop an outline of main topics and events, organized into a logical and interesting order.
- Create a first-draft storyboard and graphics to accompany it.
- Consult with an adult advisor about the first-draft storyboard.
- Create a final storyboard.
- Present the storyboard orally with accompanying graphics.
- Demonstrate knowledge of a current event by answering reasonable questions.

ASSESSMENT SCALE

4 Exceeded Expectations

3 Achieved Expectations

2 Needs Time to Achieve Expectations

1 Showed Little or No Evidence that Expectations were Achieved

	SELF	TEACHER	OTHER
PROCESS			
1. Studied a current events topic.			
2. Applied research skills to find information and cited sources.			
3. Applied writing skills to express ideas.			
4. Applied art skills to express ideas.			
5. Demonstrated creative thinking skills.			
6. Completed tasks in a timely manner.			
7. Solved problems independently.			
8. Worked cooperatively with a partner.			
9. Demonstrated a commitment to quality.			
10. Presented information effectively.			
PRODUCTS			
11. Developed an outline for the story.			
12. Composed a first-draft storyboard with at least 25 panels.			
13. Composed a final storyboard with at least 25 panels.			
14. Compiled at least 25 images for the storyboard.			
15. Coordinated images and text skillfully.			
16. Presented the storyboard orally.			
17.			
18.			
19.			
20.			
CONTENT			
21. Identified important issues and events.			
22. Organized information into a logical and interesting order.			
23. Demonstrated knowledge of a current event or issue.			
24. Analyzed the event or issue to explore reasons and results.			
25. Explained why your audience should be interested.			
26. Gave informed answers to questions.			
27.			
28.			
29.			
30.			

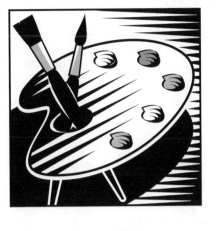

Express Yourself

Art

Do you like to draw, paint, weave, sculpt, or work with wood? People find many, many ways to be creative. But becoming an artist involves more than creativity. It also requires honing your techniques and developing an understanding of the medium in which you work,

whether it's oil paints, ink, metalworking, clay, or fabric. Learning about other artists gives further insight into style and how other artists work. And finding opportunities to exhibit your art strengthens and matures the creative process. Creating an exhibit can help you to look at your work from a different perspective in order to select your best work for display.

This project asks you to create an exhibit of original art in a medium of your choice. You will select four pieces that represent your best work and create at least one new piece. You will also explain the medium you work in and discuss some well-known artists who have worked in the same medium or who have influenced your art.

What medium do you use to express yourself?

- beadwork
- cement
- ceramic
- collage
- electronic art
- etching
- glass
- glassblowing
- ink
- leather work
- metalwork
- mosaic
- needlework
- oil paint
- origami
- pencil
- photography
- pottery
- quilting
- sculpture
- taxidermy
- video
- watercolor
- weaving
- woodwork

Project Scenario

A local art museum has decided to feature you in its Emerging Artists program. This honor is conferred upon a promising young artist who has demonstrated talent and a commitment to developing as an artist. As part of this special program, you have been selected to exhibit your work in the museum. The exhibit will include samples of your best work, along with a brochure that not only profiles two artists who have influenced your work or who use similar techniques but also a discussion of the artistic medium you prefer.

Assignment

1. Select at least four pieces of art that represent your best work. You might choose pieces because they are skillfully done, highly creative, or simply beautiful. Or you may choose pieces because they seem to express something that can't be put into words. The process of selecting your best work might be difficult, but it can also be the catalyst for new ideas or approaches that will improve and expand your artistic awareness.

2. Create at least one new piece to add to the exhibit. You may want to experiment with a new technique or improve one you already use. You might complete several new pieces before you arrive at the one you decide to exhibit. Use the creation of this new artifact to challenge and stretch your abilities. Design it to be the showpiece of your final exhibit.

3. Create a display card for each artifact. Identify the medium used, the title of the work, and your name. If your art pieces are unnamed, you will need to think of titles for them.

4. Produce an exhibit brochure. The brochure should:

- Provide a brief biography of the artist (that's you!). Give basic biographical information about yourself, but focus on your role as an artist. How did you become interested in art? Why do you choose to work in this particular medium?

- Identify two artists who work in the same medium or employ the same techniques as you do. You may profile local or well-known artists who have influenced your work. Talk with your art teacher or another established artist to help in identifying possibilities and talk through your ideas. Devote a section of the brochure to these artists. Tell who they are and give any other interesting information that you can discover through research. How do you see your work in relation to theirs?

Check It Out

Annotated Art by Robert Cumming (New York: DK, April 1995). This book provides a great introduction to looking at art. It includes social and cultural interpretations of great works of art, as well as a glossary of terms, profiles of the artists, and detailed analyses of each artwork.

Art Attack: A Short Cultural History of the Avant-Garde by Marc Aronson (New York: Clarion, 1998). This social history of twentieth-century European and American art talks about painting, poetry, music, and dance.

Learning to Look at Paintings by Mary Acton (New York: Routledge, 1997). A former art teacher discusses artistic composition, technique, and form. Includes references for further reading.

- Describe at least one technique you use when working with your favorite medium. You may need to discuss this part of the assignment with an art teacher or an experienced artist to get some ideas about describing techniques. Reading books or reviews of gallery shows or interviews with artists will also help you learn to describe artistic technique.

5. Set up your exhibit in a prearranged location so that your supervising teacher and others can view it. Be prepared to answer questions about your project.

Notes

_____
_____
_____
_____
_____
_____
_____
_____
_____
_____
_____
_____
_____
_____
_____
_____
_____
_____
_____
_____
_____

Express Yourself

STUDENT NAME _____

Artworks for possible exhibit: (Choose at least four.)

ARTWORK	MEDIUM
1. _____	_____
2. _____	_____
3. _____	_____
4. _____	_____
5. _____	_____
6. _____	_____
7. _____	_____
8. _____	_____

Possibilities for new art pieces: (Create at least one.)

ARTWORK	MEDIUM
1. _____	_____
2. _____	_____
3. _____	_____

Artists to feature in brochure: (Choose two.)

1. _____
2. _____
3. _____
4. _____

Art technique to be described in brochure: (Choose one.)

1. _____
2. _____
3. _____

Express Yourself

ASSESSMENT FORM

STUDENT NAME

Student Responsibilities

- Select at least four existing pieces of your art for display in an exhibit.
- Create at least one new piece of art for the exhibit.
- Identify and describe a favorite medium for artistic expression.
- Describe at least one technique for working with the favorite medium.
- Identify and discuss two artists who use the same medium.
- Produce a brochure, and create a display card for each piece in the exhibit.
- Set up and present an exhibit.

ASSESSMENT SCALE

4 Exceeded Expectations

3 Achieved Expectations

2 Needs Time to Achieve Expectations

1 Showed Little or No Evidence that Expectations were Achieved

	SELF	TEACHER	OTHER
PROCESS			
1. Selected four artworks you judged to be your personal best.			
2. Applied best art skills to create a new artwork.			
3. Applied research skills to find information and cited sources.			
4. Applied strong writing and layout skills to produce a brochure.			
5. Applied strong writing and layout skills to produce display cards.			
6. Interviewed an art teacher or other established artist to get information.			
7. Demonstrated a commitment to quality.			
8. Completed tasks in a timely manner.			
9. Applied problem-solving strategies.			
10. Presented an exhibit that included artwork, brochures, and display cards.			
PRODUCTS			
11. Created at least one new art piece.			
12. Made a display card for each artifact.			
13. Produced a brochure for the exhibit.			
14. Provided at least four art pieces in addition to the new work.			
15. Composed an autobiography for the brochure.			
16. Wrote a description of techniques for the brochure.			
17. Included information about two artists in the brochure.			
18.			
19.			
20.			
CONTENT			
21. Selected high-quality artworks for display.			
22. Described the medium used in making the artwork.			
23. Learned about artistic techniques used with the medium.			
24. Studied two artists who use the same medium or techniques.			
25.			
26.			
27.			
28.			
29.			
30.			

Media Master

Multimedia

Are you a computer wizard, or a techie wannabe? Or maybe you simply enjoy the interactivity of computer-based programs, CD-ROM, and Web-based information. If you've ever wanted to explore what *you* could create with a computer, this project will help you get started and put you on the road to becoming a media master.

You will need access to computers and software at your school or home to complete this project. But other than equipment, all you need to develop a simple multimedia program is comfort with computers, the ability to research, and a creative mind. After choosing the topic you want to explore and present, you will conduct research and use the software that's available to you to organize and link text, graphics, and audio.

Solutions. The company produces educational multimedia products for schools. Your job is to develop software that uses a combination of text, graphics, sound, animation, video, and other elements to inform people about a wide range of subjects. Learning Solutions is in the process of developing an entirely new line of products. You'll identify an appropriate topic and create a prototype software program that explains the topic in a multimedia presentation.

Project Scenario

You are a multimedia software design specialist who works for a company called Learning

Assignment

1. Identify the computer and software application you intend to use to develop the program. (Examples include HyperStudio, Digital

Chisel, HyperCard, and Linkway. You might also choose to create a Web-based project using software such as Claris HomePage or Adobe Pagemill.) The equipment and software you have available will help define the program that you'll create. If you are new to the technology, identify resources (books, tutorials, and people) who can help you get started. What kinds of projects can you produce using your software?

Check It Out

Creating Web Pages for Kids & Parents by Greg Holden (Foster City, CA: IDG Books, 1997). Explains how to create interesting Web pages and includes a CD-ROM with tools, templates, and clip art.

Dummies 101. This series from Wiley offers excellent guides for beginning programmers who want to learn to use a variety of software. To check out what titles are available, request a catalog.

John Wiley & Sons
Customer Care Center
10475 Crosspoint Boulevard
Indianapolis, IN 46256
1-877-762-2974

or visit their Web site:
www.wiley.com

The Help Web: A Guide to Getting Started on the Internet
www.imagescape.com/helpweb
This Web site provides information on e-mail, computer jargon, newsgroups, and more.

---

2. Choose a topic that interests you and that you feel would be effectively presented through the multimedia program you've selected. The key is to choose a topic specific enough to be fully explained in a short amount of time. (See page 126 for help in narrowing your focus.)

3. Select at least three different types of media to use in the program. For example:

Words	**Sound**
plain text	recorded sound files
hypertext	voice
	music

Images	**Movement**
clip art	movies
cartoons	animation
computer graphics	
scanned art	
photographs	

4. Conduct research to discover at least twenty pieces of information (or "facts") that you can present about your topic. (Be sure to record your sources; see pages 129–130) Think carefully how to present your information in a multimedia format. Will you present a fact as image, sound, or text? How will the information be linked?

5. Create a plan for your program. The beauty and the challenge of multimedia is that you don't have to present information in a linear fashion (moving from A to B to C, and so on). You can link A to K or even X and Y if that makes sense. You'll probably want to try different combinations. The plan for your program may take many forms:

- A set of index cards that represent computer screens; each card shows where text, graphics, "buttons," hypertext links, and so forth will be located.

- A diagram showing the links that will connect the various parts of the program.

- An outline that describes how the program will be constructed.

- Any combination of these suggestions or other methods that effectively describe your development plan.

6. Use your imagination to make the program interesting and coherent. You could present the facts in the "voice" of a character, or create a theme that draws the user through the program. Creative use of graphics, music, animation, sound, and special effects will enliven the presentation. Try to make your information as clear and as interesting as possible.

7. Once you feel your plan is strong, produce your program. Remember, you're striving to create a product that smoothly links at least twenty pieces of factual information into an educational multimedia program. As you actually do the programming, you may find that some things don't work as you planned. Be sure to revise your plan if needed.

8. Present your finished project to your supervising teacher. Arrange a time and place to present it to other audiences as well.

Notes

Media Master

GETTING STARTED

STUDENT NAME _____

Software applications I have available to develop the program:

1. _____

2. _____

People and other resources I could consult for technical advice:

1. _____

2. _____

3. _____

Topics I am interested in: (Choose one for the project.)

1. _____

2. _____

3. _____

Types of media I plan to use: (Choose at least three for the project.)

1. _____

2. _____

3. _____

4. _____

Resources I may use to find information about my topic:

1. _____

2. _____

3. _____

4. _____

Media Master
A S S E S S M E N T   F O R M

STUDENT NAME

Student Responsibilities

- Choose an appropriate topic for multimedia presentation.
- Use at least three different types of media to present information.
- Conduct research to discover at least twenty facts about the topic.
- Apply knowledge of a specific software application to develop a program.
- Create a detailed plan that shows how the program will be constructed and organized.
- Produce and present a multimedia program that effectively presents the topic.

ASSESSMENT SCALE

4 Exceeded Expectations

3 Achieved Expectations

2 Needs Time to Achieve Expectations

1 Showed Little or No Evidence that Expectations were Achieved

		SELF	TEACHER	OTHER
PROCESS	1. Chose an appropriate topic.			
	2. Selected at least three types of media to use in the program.			
	3. Conducted research to locate information about the topic.			
	4. Applied organizational skills to develop a program plan.			
	5. Applied computer skills to produce the program.			
	6. Combined knowledge of software with computer skills.			
	7. Applied best communication skills to convey meaning.			
	8. Completed tasks in a timely manner.			
	9. Applied problem-solving strategies.			
	10. Presented information effectively.			
PRODUCTS	11. Developed a comprehensive plan for the program.			
	12. Combined three types of media in creating a computer program.			
	13. Created a computer program that smoothly links twenty facts.			
	14. Created a computer program that is easy to use.			
	15.			
	16.			
	17.			
	18.			
	19.			
	20.			
CONTENT	21. Discovered and synthesized twenty facts about the topic.			
	22. Learned to use a software application for a specific task.			
	23. Demonstrated knowledge and understanding of computers.			
	24. Demonstrated understanding of the topic.			
	25.			
	26.			
	27.			
	28.			
	29.			
	30.			

Honored Athlete

Sports Statistics

People admire athletes for their physical achievements, for their ability to make strenuous activity appear easy and graceful. Not everyone who enjoys athletics is an athlete, however. Many people enjoy watching world-class athletes perform, and tracking the competitors'

performance has become an international pastime. Sports fans faithfully follow their favorite teams, discuss games, and argue passionately about which team or player is the best. For every sport, people keep statistics to track an athlete's performance throughout his or her career and to compare one athlete to the next.

This project challenges you to choose a sport and analyze the performance of several athletes by examining their statistics over a five-year period. You'll analyze the data you collect, and after evaluating your results, you will nominate one athlete to be this year's "Honored Athlete" in his or her sport.

Project Scenario

You are a statistician for *The American Athlete*, a national sports magazine. Every year the magazine publishes a special issue honoring professional athletes. Your job is to choose a sport to cover, select five outstanding athletes who have competed in the same position for at least five years, collect their performance statistics, graph your data, and analyze the results. For example, you might compare the performance statistics of five major-league baseball pitchers or five speed skaters or five LPGA golfers. After you've analyzed the statistics, you will judge the athletes' performance and assess which rates the highest overall.

You'll name this candidate the year's "Honored Athlete" in a written announcement.

Assignment

1. Decide on a sport for your project.

2. If you have selected a team sport, choose a position to focus on. (Choosing a position isn't necessary for individual sports like tennis or golf.)

3. Identify five professional athletes who have played for at least five seasons. Selecting athletes who compete in the same league or class provides the most accurate comparisons. You could, however, choose players from different eras to see if time has changed performance level, or choose some other grouping that would make interesting comparisons. Be sure to describe how you chose the athletes you're comparing (see step 9), and give a brief biographical sketch of each athlete.

4. Select at least three performance areas to evaluate and write a definition of each. Choose performance areas that are directly measurable and integral to the athlete's success. For example, for baseball pitchers, you might include games won, strikeouts, and earned run average. You wouldn't want to compare the pitchers' batting averages, since the skill is not directly related to their success as a pitchers (especially since, in some leagues, pitchers don't bat).

5. Decide on the criteria you'll use to determine who has performed the best overall. Will all your categories be equally weighted in your decision, or is one category more important than the others? In other words, spell out how you will choose your Honored Athlete.

6. Conduct your research. Design a table and record the statistics for each athlete in each category for five seasons.

7. Create graphs that visually show the performance of the athletes over the five-year period. If graphing is a new skill for you, talk with a math teacher about what types of graphs or charts are most appropriate to illustrate specific types of data. For example, when is it better to use a pie chart or a bar graph? You will create the design and style of the graphs you use, with correct labels, scales, and so forth.

Check It Out

The Math Forum: Exploring Data
www.mathforum.org/workshops/usi/dataproject
This Web site offers great resources for learning more about graphs and statistics for students of all grade levels. It includes data, lessons, and links to other Web sites.

Statistics Every Writer Should Know
www.nilesonline.com/stats
This site explains common statistics terms and the concepts behind them. Includes other useful links and resources.

8. Analyze the data you've collected and compare the performance of the athletes in each area over the five-year period.

9. Write your announcement of this year's Honored Athlete for your magazine. Include your background information on the athletes, the areas you examined, and your criteria for the award. Justify your selection by using the data to show how the athlete you've chosen has outperformed the others overall.

10. Present your finished project and be prepared to answer questions.

Honored Athlete

GETTING STARTED

STUDENT NAME

Sports I am interested in: (List three, and then choose one.)

1. _____
2. _____
3. _____

Positions (for a team sport) that I am interested in: (List three, and then choose one.)

1. _____
2. _____
3. _____

How will I select athletes? _____

_____

_____

_____

Athletes to consider: (List eight, and then select five.)

1. _____   5. _____
2. _____   6. _____
3. _____   7. _____
4. _____   8. _____

Performance areas to evaluate:

1. _____
2. _____
3. _____

Resources I could use to find information:

1. _____
2. _____

Honored Athlete

ASSESSMENT FORM

STUDENT NAME

Student Responsibilities

- Choose a sport and focus on a specific position.
- Identify five athletes who have played the position for at least five years.
- Select three performance areas to track statistics.
- Establish a method for determining best overall performance.
- Record and graph statistics for each athlete in each performance area for a five-year period.
- Determine which athlete has performed the best over a five-year span.
- Use the data to justify the choice of "Honored Athlete."
- Present the finished product.

ASSESSMENT SCALE

4 Exceeded Expectations

3 Achieved Expectations

2 Needs Time to Achieve Expectations

1 Showed Little or No Evidence that Expectations were Achieved

	SELF	TEACHER	OTHER
PROCESS			
1. Chose a sport on which to concentrate.			
2. Focused on a specific position (for a team sport).			
3. Identified five professional athletes who have played at least five years.			
4. Selected three performance areas significant to the sports position.			
5. Applied research skills to find data and cited sources.			
6. Accurately graphed data.			
7. Analyzed data to determine the best overall performance.			
8. Completed tasks in a timely manner.			
9. Applied problem-solving strategies.			
10. Presented information effectively.			
PRODUCTS			
11. Wrote a brief biography of each athlete.			
12. Produced tables and recorded statistics for each athlete.			
13. Designed a graph for performance area 1 (data for five years).			
14. Designed a graph for performance area 2 (data for five years).			
15. Designed a graph for performance area 3 (data for five years).			
16. Produced a written announcement for this year's athlete.			
17.			
18.			
19.			
20.			
CONTENT			
21. Explained criteria for selecting athletes.			
22. Composed a definition of performance area 1.			
23. Composed a definition of performance area 2.			
24. Composed a definition of performance area 3.			
25. Demonstrated knowledge and understanding of graphing.			
26. Provided statistical evidence to justify choice of honored athlete.			
27.			
28.			
29.			
30.			

Time of My Life

Survey Analysis

Have you ever wondered how much time you spend in school? How much time each day you spend waiting in line? talking on the phone? reading books? You could probably figure that out pretty easily, but could you figure out how much time you spend each year on these activities? Or how much time you'll spend on them over the next fifty years? It's amazing how many hours a person devotes to ordinary activities over a lifetime.

This project asks you to survey classmates about how they spend their time, create informative charts and graphs with data from the polls, and draw conclusions from the trends that you see in the poll results. You will also combine all of your work into a portfolio and make a presentation.

Project Scenario

A national teen magazine has asked you to help gather information for a special issue about how young people spend their time.

You've agreed to develop a poll to find out more how kids in your school spend their time. After gathering all the data, you'll analyze the results and create graphs and charts that illustrate the time people devote to specific activities. You'll also write an article evaluating the results of your poll.

Assignment

Before you begin the assignment, review the Typical School Day Poll and Activities Poll (see pages 62–63). You will use the Typical School Day Poll form to record how many minutes students your age spend on various activities on a typical weekday during the school year. You will use the Activities Poll to get more in-depth data on the activities within each category on the Typical School Day Poll.

1. Plan your survey. Think carefully about what you'd like to know, so you can write your survey to get the information that will be most useful to you. Do you want to know what activities take up the most time during a typical day? Are you more interested in school activities or leisure activities? Are you interested in how much time students spend with their families and their friends? The activity categories that you select for your poll will affect your analysis and results.

● In addition to the four activities listed on the Typical School Day Poll form (see page 62), select at least six other activities that are part of a regular weekday and record them on the form. You don't have to choose activities that happen at school; they just need to be things that students your age typically do on a school day (for example, homework, talking on the phone, chores, part-time jobs, reading, listening to music, surfing the Net, talking with a parent).

● Decide who you will survey. You must survey at least five students your age, but how will you select them? Will you select your friends? solicit volunteers? or choose them some other way? You decide how you will choose your respondents, but be sure to describe how you made that decision and think about how this will affect your results. For example, if you decide to survey the soccer team during soccer season, you'll get very different estimates of the time spent exercising than you would if you surveyed students who did not participate in athletics. (Although the survey you do will be nonscientific, you'll get better results if you increase your sample and poll more than five other students.)

2. Conduct your survey.

● Write the names of the students you are polling in the spaces on the Typical School Day Poll form (page 62), and record the answers you get. Use additional copies of the poll if you survey more students.

● Also ask each student you poll the more in-depth questions on the Activities Poll (page 63). For each category given on the poll, ask students what specific activities they take part in. Record the answers on the form.

3. Organize your results. Put the data you've collected into a form that will help you generalize your results and draw conclusions.

● Calculate the average number of minutes a day for each of the ten activities on the Typical School Day Poll. (If you need help with your calculations, be sure to ask. A calculator will make this task much easier.) Then calculate the percentage of a twenty-four-hour day that each activity consumes.

● Use the percentages you calculated to create a pie graph that shows what percentage of a day each activity represents. Since your percentages will not add up to 100%, be sure to include a category called "other." This will represent everything else students do during a typical day.

● Choose one of the activities from your Typical School Day Poll and create a bar graph that shows the number of hours each student will spend on that activity over the next fifty years. (Assume that each student does this activity *every* day—not just school days—over the next fifty years, and that the time spent on the activity remains constant.)

4. Write an article for the teen magazine, analyzing the data you collected to draw logical conclusions about the trends that you observe.

- Tell why you chose the activities for your poll, how many students you surveyed, and how you chose them.

- Explain how the characteristics of the students you polled might have affected your data.

- What did students say they would do with the time if they had an extra hour each day?

- Report your conclusions about how people your age spend their time. Include your opinions about the results of your poll.

5. Develop an interesting portfolio titled "The Time of My Life." The portfolio should contain all of the materials that you intend to submit to the magazine for publication. It should represent your best work. Use graphics, colors, and an appropriate theme to make your information visually appealing.

6. Present the portfolio to the editor (your supervising teacher) and answer relevant questions about the artifacts in it. Arrange a time and place to present your work to other audiences as well.

Check It Out

The Math Forum: Exploring Data
www.mathforum.org/workshops/usi/dataproject
This Web site offers great resources for learning more about graphs and statistics for students of all grade levels. It includes data, lessons, and links to other Web sites.

Statistics Every Writer Should Know
www.nilesonline.com/stats
This site explains common statistics terms and the concepts behind them. Includes other useful links and resources.

Notes

_____

From *Challenging Projects for Creative Minds* by Phil Schlemmer, M.Ed., and Dori Schlemmer © 1999. Free Spirit Publishing Inc., Minneapolis, MN; 800/735-7323; *www.freespirit.com*. This page may be photocopied for individual, classroom, or group work only.

Time of My Life
A TYPICAL SCHOOL DAY POLL

STUDENT NAME

Poll at least five students your age to find out how much time each day they devote to common activities. Record the number of minutes per day each person participates in each activity.

	NAME:	NAME:	NAME:	NAME:	NAME:	average minutes/day	percentage of a day
	minutes/day	minutes/day	minutes/day	minutes/day	minutes/day		
Sleeping							
Eating							
Watching TV							
Exercising							
_____							
_____							
_____							
_____							
_____							
_____							

When you have gathered all your data, calculate the average number of minutes per day students participate in each activity. Record the averages on the chart.

Then calculate what percentage of a 24-hour day the average for each activity represents. Record these percentages on the chart.

Time of My Life
ACTIVITIES POLL

For each category in the chart, ask the students you're polling what specific activities they do. Record their responses in the chart below.

	NAME:	NAME:	NAME:	NAME:	NAME:
Chores or Work					
Favorite TV Show					
Sports or Exercise					
Hobbies					
Other					
If I had one more hour a day I would. . .					

Time of My Life
A S S E S S M E N T   F O R M

STUDENT NAME

Student Responsibilities

- Create a poll to discover how much time students spend on common activities.
- Poll at least five students on how much time they devote to these common activities.
- Survey these students further to discover specific activities they engage in.
- Organize the data collected by calculating averages and percentages for each activity on the poll and displaying this information in a pie graph and a bar graph.
- Analyze the data and write a conclusion about the results of your survey.
- Develop an interesting and informative portfolio on the information.
- Present your finished product.

ASSESSMENT SCALE

4 Exceeded Expectations
3 Achieved Expectations
2 Needs Time to Achieve Expectations
1 Showed Little or No Evidence that Expectations were Achieved

	SELF	TEACHER	OTHER
PROCESS			
1. Identified at least six additional activities for the poll.			
2. Polled at least five other same-age students about each activity.			
3. Conducted an Activities Poll to get more in-depth information.			
4. Calculated average minutes per day for each activity on the poll.			
5. Calculated percentage of the day for each activity on the poll.			
6. Analyzed poll data.			
7. Drew conclusions about how students spend time.			
8. Applied charting and graphing skills.			
9. Presented information effectively.			
10.			
PRODUCTS			
11. Wrote a Typical School Day Poll.			
12. Completed a Typical School Day Poll.			
13. Completed an Activities Poll.			
14. Created a pie graph that shows the results of the poll.			
15. Created a bar graph for one activity on the poll.			
16. Wrote conclusions about how students spend time.			
17. Developed a "Time of My Life" portfolio or presentation.			
18.			
19.			
20.			
CONTENT			
21. Discovered how much time students devote to specific activities.			
22. Learned about conducting a survey.			
23. Calculated averages using the data gathered.			
24. Calculated percentages using the data gathered.			
25. Graphed data for activities on the poll.			
26. Extrapolated data to show totals over a period of time.			
27. Graphed average number of hours in fifty years for one activity.			
28.			
29.			
30.			

In Other Words

Languages

Language can be a key to understanding between people or groups, or it can be a barrier to communication. With a global economy, increasing intercontinental travel, and the diverse languages spoken by our immigrant neighbors and classmates, we need more than ever to be able to understand one another. Learning other languages helps us not only communicate but also appreciate other cultures and gain insight into our own.

This project provides an opportunity to explore a language other than your native tongue and develop a product that presents what you've learned. You don't need to be fluent in a second language to participate; you may decide to study a language you know nothing about (Japanese or Urdu, perhaps) and base the project on what you learn. Or you may work with one you already know very well. You set your goals for the project based upon your level of proficiency with the language.

This project offers a wonderful opportunity to team up with a classmate who is learning English. Your combined skills in two languages or more can help you create an exceptional presentation.

Project Scenario

You are a linguistics expert with a company that produces self-study materials for people who want to learn another language. Part of your job is to develop language-training materials and test-market them at sales shows. The president of the company has asked you to create a new high-quality product that will appeal to potential customers. You will design a product, present it to the president for approval, and then take it to the show. If you do your job well, you'll have yet another successful addition to your career portfolio.

Assignment

You have a great deal of freedom to decide what you will create. This freedom adds to the difficulty of the project. It's not easy to design a project by yourself, but the process can be very rewarding and a lot of fun, too. Planning is very important. Take time to think about a range of possibilities before deciding on a final product. Read the entire assignment carefully before you begin to develop your ideas. See page 126 for ideas on how to narrow your topic.

1. Choose a language you'd like to explore. Perhaps your school offers instruction in a variety of languages so you have teachers who can serve as resources for you. Or perhaps you can team up with another student who is learning English and create a joint project that uses two languages. Your ability with the language you choose and your access to resources will determine what kind of project you develop.

Check It Out

iLoveLanguages

www.ilovelanguages.com
This excellent Web site is really a comprehensive catalog of language-related Internet resources. Links include online language lessons, translating dictionaries, literature, translation services, software, language schools, and basic information on almost every known language. It's a wonderful place to learn about the wide variety of human language.

---

2. Decide on the audience you want to target with the product you create. If you do not know the language well, you might design a product for young children—or for other people who are just learning the language. This will allow you to focus on simple words, phrases, or even just written symbols (or letters) and sounds. If you have a good understanding of the language, you'll want to develop a more complex product that reflects your skill level.

3. Choose a product that you want to design and create. Remember, your goal in creating this product is to introduce English speakers to another language or help them become more proficient in that language. To help start your thinking process, here are some ideas of products you might consider:

- a game
- a vocabulary poster or book of phrases
- a travel guide
- a guide to celebrities
- a story or poem
- a picture book with words
- a cookbook
- a set of baseball cards
- a calendar
- a set of greeting cards
- an action comic
- an audiotape with songs or stories
- a computer program

4. When you've decided what you'll create and what that product will teach, discuss your idea with your supervising teacher to get approval. Your teacher needs to know the entire scope of your project. For example, if you decide to create a picture book, what will the pictures show? Will it be a story or will it teach vocabulary words on a specific theme? Will you include a glossary or pronunciation guide? How long will it be?

You and your supervising teacher should also discuss your current ability in the language. Will your plan be challenging enough—or too challenging? Do you need help locating people and other resources who can help you? Will you need to locate an adult fluent in your chosen language to help your supervising teacher assess your final project?

5. Plan the product by producing an outline of steps to follow. Be as precise and detailed as possible. The more you think about the project while outlining your ideas, the more likely your final product will be successful. Show the outline to your supervising teacher.

6. Follow your outline to create the final product, but remember, developing a successful product requires willingness to make revisions along the way, attention to detail, and commitment to quality.

7. Present the final product to the supervising teacher (the "president" of your company) and to others who have an interest in your work. Can you find a way to make your project available to other students?

8. Be prepared to put some additional work into your project. It is very possible that after presenting it, you and your supervising teacher will find ways to improve it.

Notes

_____

_____

_____

_____

_____

_____

_____

_____

_____

_____

_____

_____

_____

_____

In Other Words
ASSESSMENT FORM

STUDENT NAME

Student Responsibilities

- Choose a language to study for this project.
- Identify a product that can be created to demonstrate how the language is used.
- Outline a plan for producing the product.
- Create a final product.
- Present the final product and answer questions about it.

ASSESSMENT SCALE

4 Exceeded Expectations

3 Achieved Expectations

2 Needs Time to Achieve Expectations

1 Showed Little or No Evidence that Expectations were Achieved

	SELF	TEACHER	OTHER
PROCESS			
1. Chose a language to use.			
2. Identified an appropriate product to produce.			
3. Planned the steps for creating the product.			
4. Applied writing skills to express ideas.			
5. Applied art skills to express ideas.			
6. Applied research skills where necessary.			
7. Demonstrated creative-thinking skills.			
8. Completed tasks in a timely manner.			
9. Solved problems independently.			
10. Presented information effectively.			
PRODUCTS			
11. Created an outline of the plan.			
12. Created a final product.			
13. Produced the following artifacts:			
14.			
15.			
16.			
17.			
18.			
19.			
20.			
CONTENT			
21. Demonstrated knowledge of written language.			
22. Demonstrated knowledge of spoken language.			
23. Exhibited the language in its proper forms.			
24. Presented accurate information.			
25. Gave informed answers to questions.			
26.			
27.			
28.			
29.			
30.			

Great Performances

Performing Arts

The performing arts offer exciting challenges and opportunities for self-expression. As you already know, it takes practice, preparation, and hard work to do your best in a public performance—talent alone isn't enough. In order to develop and improve your skills in this area, you need opportunities to perform in public.

Great Performances sets the stage for you to showcase your performing arts skills. You will identify an area of personal interest (such as dance, figure skating, instrumental music, drama, gymnastics, vocal music, stand-up comedy, magic, or inspirational speaking), create a plan for a public performance, design a poster to advertise it, produce a program guide, arrange videotaping of the performance, and present your program to an audience.

Project Scenario

You are an artist at an entertainment company that presents shows, programs, recitals, plays, and concerts in your community. You have been invited to perform for the upcoming season. You must decide what type of performance to propose, and then develop an actual performance that you can present to audiences.

Assignment

1. Choose an area of the performing arts (or a subject that lends itself to a performance). What kind of program will you produce? What works or selections will you perform? Will you create an original work or do an interpretation of an existing work?

2. Create a plan for the program:

● Give your program a descriptive title.

● Identify three distinct parts or segments for your program. For example, you may decide to present three acts or three songs or three recitations or even three different types of performances (such as a dance, a piano piece, and a poetry reading).

● Develop an outline to show how the three parts of the program will be presented and provide details about each part.

● List the resources you'll need for the performance. What supplies, equipment, and props will you need? Do you need the help of other artists? What kind of performance space do you require?

3. Discuss your plan with your supervising teacher to ensure that the performance is feasible. Can you get all the resources that you will need? Run through your anticipated program several times, getting feedback from your supervising teacher and others. Is the performance too long? too short? Are any techniques or portions of the performance not working as you'd like? Use the feedback you receive to make the necessary adjustments to your program.

4. Set a date, time, and place to present your program. This must be approved by your supervising teacher.

5. Design an attractive, informative poster advertising your program. Use the title as a heading. Describe the program in enough detail that people who see the poster will know what to expect. Be sure to include *who, what, when,* and *where.*

6. Compose a one-page program guide for the audience. The program guide should provide a brief biography of the performer(s) and describe what will be presented.

7. Practice the program until it is ready to present. This may be the most time-consuming and difficult part of this project.

8. Arrange to have the program videotaped so that you have a permanent record of your performance.

9. Present your program to your audience.

Notes

_____

_____

_____

_____

_____

_____

_____

Great Performances

GETTING STARTED

Title of show: _____

Area of the performing arts: _____

Program segments:

1. _____

2. _____

3. _____

(Write a detailed outline of program segments on the back or on a separate sheet of paper.)

What equipment, props, or accompanists do you need to arrange?

_____

_____

Possible dates for presentation:

1. _____   Location: _____

2. _____   _____

3. _____   Time: _____

Who may be able to videotape the performance? Whose equipment will be used?

_____

_____

_____

Great Performances

ASSESSMENT FORM

STUDENT NAME

Student Responsibilities

- Focus on one area of the performing arts.
- Create a plan that includes a descriptive title, three program segments, and a detailed outline.
- Arrange a date, time, and place for the program to be presented.
- Design an attractive, informative poster to advertise the program.
- Produce a one-page program guide.
- Present the program to an audience and have it videotaped for a permanent record.

ASSESSMENT SCALE

4 Exceeded Expectations

3 Achieved Expectations

2 Needs Time to Achieve Expectations

1 Showed Little or No Evidence that Expectations were Achieved

	SELF	TEACHER	OTHER
PROCESS			
1. Chose the type of performance to present and selected appropriate works.			
2. Developed a plan for the program.			
3. Discussed the plan with a supervising teacher.			
4. Established a date, time, and place for the program.			
5. Applied best art/graphic design skills.			
6. Applied best writing skills.			
7. Practiced the program to prepare for presentation.			
8. Completed tasks in a timely manner.			
9. Applied problem-solving strategies.			
10. Delivered an effective performance.			
PRODUCTS			
11. Produced an outline that describes the program.			
12. Designed an attractive, informative poster.			
13. Created a one-page program guide.			
14. Arranged to have the final program videotaped.			
15. Presented the program to an audience.			
16.			
17.			
18.			
19.			
20.			
CONTENT			
21. Selected appropriate works to perform.			
22. Increased proficiency in one area of the performing arts.			
23. Learned how to organize a personal performance.			
24. Presented an entertaining performance.			
25.			
26.			
27.			
28.			
29.			
30.			

Local Hero

Journalism

When you think of heroes, do you immediately think of legendary warriors, people in your history books, entertainers, or important leaders in the news? Have you ever looked closer to home? Women and men living in your city or neighborhood have made

important contributions to the community and have heroically faced challenges to make their world a better place. Some of these people are well known; others have stories just waiting to be told. There might be a local politician or business person who had the courage to bring about positive change, or a young woman who trains Seeing Eye dogs so that people who are blind can be more independent, or a dad who coaches Little League and serves as a role model for hundreds of kids, or someone who has dedicated hours and hours toward making a bicycle trail become a reality. Many people work quietly in the background to make a difference—doctors, grandparents, educators, volunteers, and young people.

This project invites you to identify someone in your community whom you admire and consider a local hero. You'll gather information about that person, conduct interviews, and produce an article that could be published in a newspaper.

Project Scenario

You are seeking a job as a journalist with a local newspaper. To assess your abilities, the editor has asked you to submit an article for an upcoming feature called "Local Heroes." The feature will focus on community heroes: people from the area who are positive role models and have contributed to the community in some way. The editor wants you to identify a hero in your community and write an article about the person following the newspaper's guidelines. Your article should define the word *hero,* offer a brief biographical profile, and describe the qualities and accomplishments of the hero you've selected. The editor has also asked you to supply two photographs or illustrations with captions to accompany the article. An interesting, well-written article submitted by the assigned deadline will guarantee you a personal interview with the editor.

Assignment

1. Develop a written definition of a local hero. How can you tell when someone in the community is a hero? Talk with friends, family members, and teachers to determine what qualities a hero has. You might even ask one of your teachers if you could lead a class discussion to find out what your classmates think a hero is.

2. Identify someone in your community who fits your definition of a local hero. Once again, ask for suggestions from friends, classmates, family members, neighbors, and teachers. Watch the local news, listen to local radio stations, contact local newspapers, or visit the library to get ideas. Remember, you must be able to show how this person fits your definition of a hero.

3. Set up an interview with the person you've selected to profile. (See page 135 for guidelines on interviews.) Prepare your questions in advance so you can refer to them during the interview—and so you don't forget to ask for important information. When conducting the interview, take careful notes, and, if possible, record the interview on audiotape or videotape for future reference. Be sure to get approval for this interview from your supervising teacher

Check It Out

How to Write a News Article by Michael Kronenwetter (New York: Franklin Watts, 1995). Written for kids in grades 7–12, this valuable book discusses the basic aspects of news journalism, including judging what is newsworthy, gathering information, journalistic ethics and bias, and shaping a story.

My Hero
www.myhero.com
This Web site offers inspiring true stories about heroes of all kinds—teachers, artists, writers, athletes, explorers, scientists, business leaders, freedom fighters, parents, and even animals. Visitors can read the stories, or submit their own.

The Write Site
www.writesite.org
This journalism site has a great range of resources for students, including Newsroom, which guides you through investigating, planning, and writing news stories.

and your parent or guardian. It is important that they know where and when you are meeting, and with whom.

4. Collect at least two photographs of the hero to include in your article. You may take the photos yourself or ask your subject to supply photos. (Or you may create drawings instead of photographs, if you prefer.)

5. Interview at least one other person who knows the hero or has firsthand knowledge of his or her accomplishments. You may tape this interview or just take notes. Again, be sure to get approval for this interview from your supervising teacher and parent or guardian.

6. From your interview notes, develop an outline for your article. Write a first-draft article about the hero, remembering to cover what's known as the five Ws: who, what, when, where, and why. Also write captions describing the photographs (or illustrations) that will accompany your article. Ask a friend or parent to read it and then sit down with you to discuss it. Think about the feedback you get to find ways the article could be changed and improved. Do you need to gather more information or edit and refine what you have? It is also a good idea to let the hero review the article to check for accuracy.

7. Produce your final article. The article should include these things:

- a definition of a hero

- a brief biography of the hero you have identified

- an explanation of why the person is a hero

- at least one specific example of this person's heroism

- at least two photographs or illustrations of the hero

- a caption for each photograph (captions should provide interesting information about the hero).

8. Turn in your completed article on or before the assigned deadline. (Set deadline date with supervising teacher.)

9. Present your finished article and be prepared to answer questions about your work.

Notes

_____

_____

_____

_____

_____

_____

_____

_____

_____

_____

_____

_____

_____

_____

_____

_____

Local Hero
GETTING STARTED

SAMPLE INTERVIEW QUESTIONS:

1. How did you first get interested or involved in your work?

2. What are some things you've learned through your experience?

3. What advice do you have for young people as they go to school, choose careers, and get involved in their communities?

4. What is the most interesting or challenging part of your work?

5. What is your definition of a hero?

YOUR INTERVIEW QUESTIONS:

The questions you write for your interview will depend on your hero and his or her accomplishments. Try to think of many questions and then choose what you consider to be the best ones for your interview. You may think of follow-up questions during the interview that you would like to ask.

_____

_____

_____

_____

_____

_____

_____

_____

_____

_____

_____

_____

_____

_____

Local Hero

A S S E S S M E N T   F O R M

STUDENT NAME

Student Responsibilities

- Define *hero.*
- Identify a local hero who fits the definition developed.
- Interview the hero (take notes and record on audiotape or videotape).
- Photograph or illustrate the hero and write captions.
- Interview someone who knows the hero.
- Write a first- and final-draft article about the hero.
- Present your finished product.

ASSESSMENT SCALE	
4	Exceeded Expectations
3	Achieved Expectations
2	Needs Time to Achieve Expectations
1	Showed Little or No Evidence that Expectations were Achieved

		SELF	TEACHER	OTHER
PROCESS	**1.** Solicited opinions about "heroism."			
	2. Identified a local hero.			
	3. Conducted an interview with the hero.			
	4. Interviewed a second person about the hero.			
	5. Applied best writing skills.			
	6. Participated in at least one editing conference.			
	7. Completed tasks in a timely manner.			
	8. Applied problem-solving strategies.			
	9. Applied technology skills (photography, AV taping).			
	10. Presented information effectively.			
PRODUCTS	**11.** Developed a definition of a hero.			
	12. Recorded an interview with a hero in writing and on audiotape or videotape.			
	13. Recorded a second interview in writing or on tape.			
	14. Collected at least two photographs (or created at least two illustrations) of the hero.			
	15. Produced an appropriate caption for each photograph.			
	16. Wrote a first-draft article.			
	17. Composed a final-draft article incorporating feedback from review.			
	18.			
	19.			
	20.			
CONTENT	**21.** Learned about heroism and how it is recognized.			
	22. Discovered biographical information about the hero.			
	23. Studied at least one heroic event or situation.			
	24. Justified the selection of the hero.			
	25. Presented accurate information.			
	26. Answered questions about the article.			
	27.			
	28.			
	29.			
	30.			

Now Presenting

Conference Planning

Conferences offer an opportunity for people who share common interests to get together as a group to explore specific issues. Almost all trade organizations and academic disciplines put on conferences to keep their members informed about what is currently happening in the profession. There are annual conferences on food safety, school violence, product packaging, human rights, smoking, fundraising, mathematics, economics—you name it. There are even conferences about putting on conferences successfully!

This project allows you to organize a mini-conference for students in your school. You will choose the theme for the conference, identify possible topics, schedule the conference, organize speakers, promote the conference, and serve as the facilitator.

Project Scenario

You are a consultant for Conferences Unlimited, a company that coordinates and presents educational conferences and workshops. Conferences Unlimited recently received a request to help organize a conference at a local school, and you've been named project director.

Your job is to develop the theme for the conference and make sure that everything is well planned and smoothly presented. You will achieve a successful conference by choosing a theme that students will see as useful or interesting, enlisting speakers who know how to talk so that kids listen, and ensuring that all the necessary logistical arrangements have been made.

Assignment

1. Choose a theme for the conference that will attract students. For example, if you have the conference in the spring, you might choose "Summer Opportunities for Students: Work, Recreation, and Learning." You can also organize a conference to address specific problems or concerns. A conference called "Respecting Our Differences" could include speakers who talk about how to get along with each other, creating a mediation program, and strategies for coping with stress.

2. Justify your choice of theme in writing. Answer the question "How do you know students will be interested in this theme?" and back up your opinions with facts.

3. Meet with your supervising teacher to set a date and time for the conference and to decide on where it can be held.

4. Prepare a list of three specific topics that relate to the conference theme. Each topic will be the focus of a presentation at the conference. Ask for suggestions from teachers, parents, friends, and classmates to help identify the best possible topics.

5. Recruit at least three speakers to present at the conference. Each presentation will focus on one of the topics and last about ten to fifteen minutes. (Speakers may be classmates or adults, or you may be one of the speakers if you wish.) Be sure to inform your speakers of the date and time and place of the conference, and to reconfirm their presentation plans.

You could also decide to have one main keynote speaker for everyone to hear, then offer several smaller "break-out" sessions where students attend the topic of their choice. This option involves more planning, organization and space, but it may be a format that works for you. Get other people's opinions before deciding.

6. Create an agenda for your conference. Decide on the best order of presentation. Which presenter should go first? Who should go next? Who would be best at the end? Will you create a schedule for people who attend the conference?

7. Advertise the conference. Choose the most effective method for getting the word out— poster, flier, announcements at school or on the radio. Your ad should include:

- The conference title (clearly identifying the theme).

- A brief statement of purpose: Why are you holding this conference and why should anyone be interested?

- The conference schedule: date, time, place, list of presenters, and topics to be covered.

- A credit to the organizer: "This conference is brought to you by (your name)."

8. Set up the conference. Arrange for rooms, plan the traffic flow, check in with presenters to make sure they are prepared and to identify any special equipment or other needs (an overhead projector, a table, water, etc.).

9. Facilitate the conference. Begin by explaining the theme and its importance to the audience. Introduce each presenter before he or she speaks, and offer a wrap-up statement at the end by thanking the presenters for participating, and the audience for attending. (For tips on public speaking, see page 136.)

10. Prepare an evaluation form that lets attendees evaluate the conference. Ask attendees to complete this form, and use the information you receive to help you reflect on your experience.

Now Presenting

GETTING STARTED

STUDENT NAME

List two possible themes: (Choose one for the conference.)

1. _____

Why is this interesting to the audience? _____

_____

2. _____

Why is this interesting to the audience? _____

_____

List six topics that relate to your chosen theme: (Choose three for the conference.)

1. _____ 4. _____

2. _____ 5. _____

3. _____ 6. _____

List possible dates for the conference: (Choose one with the approval of your supervising teacher.)

1. _____ 3. _____

2. _____ 4. _____

List six possible speakers: (Choose three for the conference.)

1. _____ 4. _____

2. _____ 5. _____

3. _____ 6. _____

Questions I have at this point: _____

_____

_____

_____

_____

_____

_____

Now Presenting
ASSESSMENT FORM

STUDENT NAME

Student Responsibilities

- Choose a conference theme and explain why it's interesting and relevant to students.
- Arrange a date, time, and place for the conference.
- Identify three topics closely related to the theme and recruit speakers to present.
- Develop an agenda for the conference and advertise the conference.
- Facilitate the conference by making a brief initial presentation, introducing speakers, etc.
- Write an evaluation form and ask attendees to fill it out.

ASSESSMENT SCALE

4 Exceeded Expectations

3 Achieved Expectations

2 Needs Time to Achieve Expectations

1 Showed Little or No Evidence that Expectations were Achieved

	SELF	TEACHER	OTHER
PROCESS			
1. Chose a meaningful and interesting conference theme.			
2. Developed a rationale for choosing the theme.			
3. Applied organizational skills.			
4. Identified three topics that relate to the conference theme.			
5. Recruited three speakers to present at the conference.			
6. Applied best writing skills.			
7. Applied best graphic design skills for the advertisement.			
8. Facilitated the conference effectively and smoothly.			
9. Completed tasks in a timely manner.			
10. Applied problem-solving strategies.			
PRODUCTS			
11. Justified the theme choice in writing.			
12. Created an agenda for the conference.			
13. Produced an interesting, carefully designed advertisement that drew people to the conference.			
14. Made sure presenters had all the materials they needed.			
15. Presented a well-organized, thematic conference.			
16. Created an effective evaluation form.			
17.			
18.			
19.			
20.			
CONTENT			
21. Identified a thematic area that is relevant to students.			
22. Discovered three topics that relate to the conference theme.			
23. Selected appropriate presenters.			
24. Presented an educational, thought-provoking conference.			
25. Analyzed the feedback from the evaluation forms.			
26.			
27.			
28.			
29.			
30.			

The Time Traveler

Popular Culture

Although you might suspect this project is about history, it really involves thinking critically about your current world and life. What would a traveler from the future see if he or she visited your hometown today? How would the time traveler view your daily life?

What would this person collect to bring back to the future to show people what life in your hometown was like?

In this project, you will become that time traveler. And in that role, your task is to investigate "what life was like" at the beginning of the twenty-first century. What did kids your age do and think about as they grew up? What was family life like? What issues were people dealing with? How did people dress, wear their hair, spend their free time? What important national and international events affected their lives? The purpose of this project is for you to demonstrate your understanding of your world.

Project Scenario

You are a student in the year 2199. Your class has just completed a unit on genealogy and each student has traced a branch of his or her family tree back to the early twenty-first century. You've discovered a great-great-great-great-great-grandparent who grew up in your hometown at the beginning of the twenty-first century. For your final assignment you enter a time machine and travel to that time period where you can observe history first-hand. Your assignment is to observe the everyday life of your ancestor and analyze the cultural influences in his or her life. Returning to 2199, you create a presentation based on what you learned about your ancestor's world.

From *Challenging Projects for Creative Minds* by Phil Schlemmer, M.Ed., and Dori Schlemmer © 1999. Free Spirit Publishing Inc., Minneapolis, MN; 800/735-7323; *www.freespirit.com*. This page may be photocopied for individual, classroom, or group work only.

Assignment

To complete this assignment effectively, imagine the character of the time traveler that you'll become. Who are you? What is your life like in 2199? What is important to you? As a student from the future traveling back in time, you'll complete the following:

1. Keep a journal to record your observations about your visit to the past. Make notes over a four-week period. (Remember, you live in 2199, so write your entries in the voice of an observer from that time.) Your journal should show the natural curiosity of someone visiting a world two hundred years past, analyzing even the most apparently common actions and behaviors. Try to be as creative and insightful as possible.

2. Develop a scrapbook about life at the turn of the millennium. Include materials such as newspaper clippings, magazine articles, family pictures, or souvenirs from your ancestor's school, and write explanations for each item in the scrapbook. Cover a variety of events and observations that show what people did or thought about during this time period, and organize your scrapbook thematically (fashion, news headlines, entertainment, primitive technology, for example). You may devote more space to an idea or issue that you find particularly interesting that touches on key events in your ancestor's life.

3. Select five or more "original artifacts" from this time period to display in your final exhibit. Chose objects you think show something significant about this time period. Write a description of each object, explaining what it is, how it was used, and how it relates to life in 2199. Does the device seem primitive? Is it merely a charming antique or does it have further significance? Does it represent an obsolete era or does it have relevance in today's

world? What insights does the object give into life in your ancestor's time?

4. Choose one of the following options:

a) Write an essay on life at the turn of the millennium. Was this a good time to be growing up? Why or why not? What kinds of problems existed and how have those problems affected life in 2199? This should be a thoughtful essay based not only on your current life in 2199, but also on facts you learned throughout your visit to the past. Use specific examples to illustrate your points, and think of a good title for your essay. After you've written the first draft, ask several people to read it and offer suggestions for improving it. Incorporate helpful suggestions into your final draft.

b) Design a visual display that tells something about your visit. You might create a photo documentary, poster, mural, collage, painting, drawings, or time line of events. Include brief captions, commentary, or explanations so people can quickly understand what your visual presentation shows. Once you've chosen what you will display, study examples of this type of visual format to get ideas of what is effective or pleasing.

c) Prepare an oral presentation about your visit to present to your classmates upon your return from your time travels. If you've ever visited a museum and heard a tour guide explain an exhibit, you've seen an example of an interpretive oral presentation. An effective oral presentation is lively and interesting. You want to avoid droning on and on, giving fact after fact, until people nod off or wander away. Capture your audience's attention by asking a question, using props, telling a story that makes a point, adding humor or audience participation. Ask friends and teachers about effective presentations they've heard.

d) Perhaps you enjoy acting and would like to create a dramatic reenactment of your visit. Outline your skit, writing out your lines and describing what you will do. Be sure to include any props or costumes that will enhance your delivery. And practice, practice, practice.

e) You could produce a videotape, computer presentation, or slide show about your project. Show original footage of your trip and scenes from your ancestor's life: a trip to the grocery store (an ancient way of procuring food), the home (simple by modern standards; no computerized wallpaper or atomizing waste recycler), a visit to an entertainment vendor called "the video store" (videotapes were crude, rectangular information-storage devices that were collected in special buildings; people had to leave their homes in gas-guzzling vehicles and wander aimlessly down aisles in search of something to occupy their time later that evening).

5. Assemble and present your final exhibit. Plan to make your journal, scrapbook, original artifacts and fourth component accessible to viewers. Make a sign or poster that welcomes or introduces people to your exhibit. Be prepared to answer questions about items in the exhibit.

Notes

_____
_____
_____
_____
_____
_____
_____
_____
_____
_____
_____
_____
_____
_____
_____
_____

The Time Traveler

ASSESSMENT FORM

STUDENT NAME

Student Responsibilities

- Observe the world of the early twenty-first century from the perspective of a visitor from the future.
- Keep a journal that describes and analyzes daily life for four weeks.
- Produce a scrapbook that explains or illustrates topics of interest.
- Select five or more "original artifacts" to describe and display.
- Create a fourth component for your presentation: an essay; visual display; or oral, dramatic, or multimedia presentation.
- Develop and present an exhibit that creatively shows what you've learned.
- Demonstrate knowledge of your exhibit by answering reasonable questions.

ASSESSMENT SCALE

4 Exceeded Expectations

3 Achieved Expectations

2 Needs Time to Achieve Expectations

1 Showed Little or No Evidence that Expectations were Achieved

	SELF	TEACHER	OTHER
PROCESS			
1. Observed daily local events for at least four weeks.			
2. Adopted the "voice" of a person from the future.			
3. Analyzed current culture.			
4. Solved problems independently.			
5. Demonstrated creative thinking skills.			
6. Completed tasks in a timely manner.			
7. Applied art skills to express ideas visually.			
8. Applied writing skills to express ideas in words.			
9. Presented information effectively.			
10. Demonstrated a commitment to quality.			
PRODUCTS			
11. Produced a four-week daily journal.			
12. Developed a "turn-of-the-millennium" scrapbook.			
13. Selected and described at least five "original artifacts."			
14. Created a fourth component for exhibit: _____.			
15. Combined materials to create an exhibit.			
16. Produced a well-organized exhibit.			
17.			
18.			
19.			
20.			
CONTENT			
21. Analyzed life at the beginning of the twenty-first century.			
22. Focused on specific aspects of popular culture to create a coherent presentation.			
23. Shared insight on the present time and current trends.			
24. Gave informed answers to questions.			
25.			
26.			
27.			
28.			
29.			
30.			

The Desktop Publisher
Magazine Publishing

With readily available personal computers and software, many people have become self-publishers, putting together newsletters, magazines, or promotional materials from their school or their home office. With the proper equipment and some practice, virtually anyone can produce professional-looking publications.

This project provides an opportunity for you to become a desktop publisher. You and two or three classmates will use computers to design, lay out, and produce one issue of a magazine. The magazine will focus on topics that are interesting or important to people your age.

Your magazine production team will need a computer with word processing and graphics software, as well as a printer. You might find additional publishing tools such as scanners, digital cameras, clip art files, and Internet resources useful, too. Recruiting an advisor who has desktop publishing experience is highly recommended.

Project Scenario

Quality Press, a magazine publishing company, sponsors an annual competition to motivate students to try their hand at actually producing a magazine. The competition is called DTP-4U, Desktop Publishing for:

1. Useful Skills
2. Unique Products
3. Undeniable Quality
4. Ultimate Success

You and two or three colleagues have decided to enter. Your task is to follow competition guidelines to produce a high-quality magazine on a desktop computer. Your goal is to learn about desktop publishing as you pursue topics of personal interest. If you win the contest, your magazine will be published as an insert in one of Quality Press's upcoming issues, and every student in your school will receive a free copy.

Assignment

1. Form a publication team of three or four members.

2. Brainstorm ideas and decide on a theme for your magazine. All team members should agree on the theme. Here are some examples:

- Animals
- Celebrities
- Culture
- Current events
- Entertainment
- Ancient civilizations
- History
- Hobbies
- Local issues
- Poetry
- Science fiction
- School news
- Social activism
- Space
- Sports
- Technology
- The environment
- Weather

3. Brainstorm ideas and decide on a title for your magazine.

4. Examine sample issues of various magazines to get ideas for yours. Look at how they are organized, what features they contain, and how information is presented.

5. Most magazines contain two basic types of articles: (1) *regular columns* that will appear in every issue, and (2) *feature stories* that cover a topic of current interest to readers. Decide how many regular columns and feature stories your magazine will include; each team member should plan to write at least one article of each type.

6. Follow the Author's Checklist (see page 88) to write the regular columns for the magazine. Each article must relate to the focus of your magazine, but you may select any genre that might be appropriate. For example:

- Opinion
- Humor
- Essay
- Poetry
- Short Story
- Interview
- Reviews
- Quizzes
- Puzzles
- Comics

Give each regular column of your magazine an appropriate and interesting title.

7. Follow the Author's Checklist (see page 88) to write your feature articles for the magazine. Each current feature should focus on a specific topic and be written as an informative article based on research and facts.

8. Agree on a design for your magazine. How many pages will it be? What will the finished dimensions be? How will the cover look? Will the magazine contain illustrations, photographs, color, or distinctive treatment of the type? What typefaces will you use? How will articles be laid out on the page?

9. Follow the Production Checklist (see page 89) to produce a finished magazine.

10. Submit the magazine to your managing editor (supervising teacher) for final approval.

11. Present your finished project.

Check It Out

Desktop Publishing: The Art of Communication by John Madama (Minneapolis: Lerner, 1993). Covers all aspects of desktop publishing— including computer hardware and software, typography, design, layout, and printing—to guide teens in the techniques for producing their own publications.

The Desktop Publisher
AUTHOR'S CHECKLIST

Author's Name: _____

Indicate which type of article this checklist is for, then write your genre or topic on the appropriate line before completing each item on the list.

☐ Regular Column

    What kind of column is it? (e.g., interview, editorial, review) _____

    Topic _____

☐ Feature Article

    Topic _____

To prepare this article for publication, I . . .

☐ Decided on a genre and/or specific topic to fit the magazine's theme.

☐ Conducted necessary research.

☐ Produced a first-draft article.

☐ Had a conference to discuss the first-draft article with a team member.

☐ Revised the first-draft article after input from the conference.

☐ Edited the revised draft for grammar, spelling, and punctuation.

☐ Developed at least one graphic (illustration, photograph, clip art, or distinctive title treatment) to add visual interest to the article.

☐ Had a conference with a teacher or other adult advisor to discuss the revised article.

☐ Made additional revisions as needed.

☐ Conducted additional research when necessary.

☐ Published a final draft of the article with at least one graphic.

The Desktop Publisher

PRODUCTION CHECKLIST

Team Member 1: _____   Team Member 3: _____

Team Member 2: _____   Team Member 4: _____

Magazine Theme: _____

Title: _____

Audience: (Who will be interested in reading this magazine? Be as specific as possible.) _____

_____

☐ Regular columns that will appear in each issue:

(Attach Author's Checklist for each column.)

Title: _____   Team member responsible: _____

Description: _____

_____

Title: _____   Team member responsible: _____

Description: _____

_____

Title: _____   Team member responsible: _____

Description: _____

_____

Title: _____   Team member responsible: _____

Description: _____

_____

continued on next page. . .

☐ Feature articles that will appear in the first issue of the magazine:

(Attach Author's Checklist for each column.)

Title: _____   Team member responsible: _____

Description: _____

Title: _____   Team member responsible: _____

Description: _____

Title: _____   Team member responsible: _____

Description: _____

Title: _____   Team member responsible: _____

Description: _____

☐ Developed an appealing format for the magazine:

Size: _____

Number of pages: _____

Number and kind of illustrations: _____

Number of photographs: _____

Color or black and white? _____

Typeface(s) for titles and headlines: _____

Typeface(s) for articles: _____

Where will page numbers appear? _____

☐ Created an appealing cover.

☐ Produced a table of contents.

The Desktop Publisher

ASSESSMENT FORM

STUDENT NAME

Student Responsibilities

- Write a regular column following the Author's Checklist.
- Create a graphic that supports the regular column.
- Write a feature article following the Author's Checklist.
- Create a graphic that supports the feature article's topic.
- Combine his or her work with the other team members' work.
- Publish a magazine following the Production Checklist.
- Present the finished project.

ASSESSMENT SCALE

4 Exceeded Expectations

3 Achieved Expectations

2 Needs Time to Achieve Expectations

1 Showed Little or No Evidence that Expectations were Achieved

		SELF	TEACHER	OTHER
PROCESS	1. Assembled a magazine publishing team.			
	2. Participated in developing a theme and title for the magazine.			
	3. Examined various magazines for organizational ideas.			
	4. Conducted the necessary research for each article and included source citations.			
	5. Worked cooperatively as a team member.			
	6. Used available technology to produce a magazine.			
	7. Applied best desktop publishing skills.			
	8. Used the Author's Checklist (writing process).			
	9. Used the Production Checklist (publishing process).			
	10. Presented information effectively.			
PRODUCTS	11. Wrote a regular column article.			
	12. Created a graphic for the regular column article.			
	13. Followed and completed an Author's Checklist for the regular column article.			
	14. Wrote a feature article.			
	15. Created a graphic for the feature article.			
	16. Followed and completed an Author's Checklist for the feature article.			
	17. Developed a design and format for the magazine.			
	18. Completed a Production Checklist.			
	19. Designed and produced a cover and table of contents for the magazine.			
	20. Published a magazine.			
CONTENT	21. Identified the theme and audience for the magazine.			
	22. Chose an appropriate topic for the regular column.			
	23. Included accurate information in the regular column.			
	24. Designed a graphic that supports the regular column.			
	25. Chose an appropriate topic for the feature article.			
	26. Included accurate information in the feature article.			
	27. Designed a graphic that supports the feature article.			
	28.			
	29.			
	30.			

Sports Specialist

Athletic Training

Professional athletes and coaches aren't the only people dedicated to sports. Trainers, sportswriters, announcers, physical therapists, and kinesiologists (who study human movement) all have found other ways to integrate athletics into their professional lives. They bring valuable knowledge and skills to the world of sports.

This project allows you an opportunity to become one of these sports specialists. You will choose a sport and investigate methods athletes could use to improve their skills, strength, and stamina. You will study an athlete who has been successful in the sport and design a training program that other athletes could follow to improve their performance.

Project Scenario

You are a sports specialist who designs training programs for young athletes. You help individual athletes who want to improve their performance in specific sports. When an athlete or a coach requests a training program, you provide a Training Program Manual that lists the necessary skills, describes practice drills that will help the athlete develop those skills, and recommends exercises to increase strength and stamina. You also offer a motivational essay about a famous athlete to explain how he or she made it to the top of the sport.

Assignment

1. Choose a sport to study and, if you wish, a specific position or specialty area within that sport (for example, a soccer goalie or a giant-slalom skier).

2. Identify three reputable sources of information about the sport. At least one source must be a coach or physical education teacher. Make arrangements to interview this person (after getting approval from your supervising teacher and a parent or guardian). Describe your project and ask for help and information about each part of the assignment. Other sources might include books, magazines, and Web sites.

Check It Out

Aerobics and Fitness Association of America
15250 Ventura Boulevard, Suite 200
Sherman Oaks, CA 91403
1-877-968-7263
www.afaa.com
AFAA is a national organization for aerobics instructors and personal trainers.

National Athletic Trainers' Association
2952 Stemmons Freeway
Dallas, TX 75247
1-800-879-6282
www.nata.org
NATA is the professional association for Certified Athletic Trainers, whose goal is to improve the quality of training for athletes.

National Strength and Conditioning Association
1955 N. Union Boulevard
Colorado Springs, CO 80909
(719) 632-6722
www.nsca-lift.org
This organization is the authority on strength and conditioning for improving athletic performance. Personal trainers and strength coaches can become certified by the NSCA.

3. Using the sources you identified, produce a list of necessary skills for the sport, position, or specialty area. You must include at least three skills.

4. Describe at least one practice drill for each skill, using illustrations or photographs as necessary.

5. Recommend a set of strength and stamina exercises for an athlete in the sport you've chosen, and describe how each exercise is done. Include a minimum of five exercises. Avoid common exercises like jumping jacks, push-ups, and sit-ups; concentrate on exercises recommended by the coach you interview.

6. Create a chart or table to display the names of exercises, the muscles they benefit, a suggested regimen, and a brief explanation of why an athlete in this sport needs each exercise. (See Exercise Table on page 94.)

7. Profile a well-known athlete who has made it to the top of your chosen sport. Do research to find out how that athlete trained and what special skills he or she needed to develop. How does this person maintain a competitive edge?

8. Compile the finished materials into the Training Program Manual for your client. Include a bibliography that cites all of your sources. (See pages 129–130.)

9. Present your finished project.

Sports Specialist
GETTING STARTED

Use this form to begin organizing your information for assignment step #6.

EXERCISE TABLE

NAME OF EXERCISE	WHICH MUSCLES	SUGGESTED REGIMEN	REASON FOR EXERCISE

Sports Specialist
ASSESSMENT FORM

STUDENT NAME

Student Responsibilities

- Identify three sources of information about a specific sport.
- Contact and interview at least one coach or physical education instructor.
- Describe skills and practice drills in writing and with illustrations.
- Describe strength and stamina exercises and make a table detailing each.
- Compose an essay about a famous athlete.
- Produce a Training Program Manual that includes all of the above information.
- Present the finished project.

ASSESSMENT SCALE

4 Exceeded Expectations
3 Achieved Expectations
2 Needs Time to Achieve Expectations
1 Showed Little or No Evidence that Expectations were Achieved

		SELF	TEACHER	OTHER
PROCESS	1. Chose a sport, position, or specialty area to study.			
	2. Identified three sources of information about the sport.			
	3. Contacted/interviewed at least one coach or PE instructor.			
	4. Conducted research to discover important skills and drills, and cited sources.			
	5. Conducted research to discover effective exercises, and cited sources.			
	6. Conducted research to learn about a famous athlete, and cited sources.			
	7. Applied best writing skills.			
	8. Completed tasks in a timely manner.			
	9. Applied problem-solving strategies.			
	10. Presented information effectively.			
PRODUCTS	11. Developed a list of skills for the sport (three or more).			
	12. Produced written descriptions and illustrations for the practice drills.			
	13. Produced written descriptions and illustrations for at least five strength and stamina exercises.			
	14. Created a table to show exercises, benefits, etc.			
	15. Developed a written profile of a well-known athlete.			
	16. Produced a Training Program Manual.			
	17.			
	18.			
	19.			
	20.			
CONTENT	21. Identified key skills needed in the sport.			
	22. Learned about skill development techniques.			
	23. Discovered methods of building strength and stamina.			
	24. Learned about a well-known athlete, and communicated what was learned.			
	25.			
	26.			
	27.			
	28.			
	29.			
	30.			

Let Me Illustrate

Book Design and Illustration

Good authors describe scenes, characters, and settings so vividly that readers feel as if they can see the story. When you first heard the story of Rapunzel, couldn't you just envision the young woman in the tower with her waves of hair cascading out the window and down to the ground? You can probably still remember what you imagined as a child when someone read that story to you.

This project asks you to select a challenging book to read, illustrate scenes from the story, and write intriguing copy for its book jacket (what you read to help you decide if you want to read the book). You'll also write a caption and a descriptive paragraph for each illustration you create. Choose this project only if you enjoy reading, like to write, and want to produce a collection of drawings or paintings.

Project Scenario

You are a freelance artist and writer. An editor from a publishing company wants you to work on a special project. The publisher is planning a new edition of a popular book and wants you to create a dynamic book jacket and illustrations for it. You've been asked to produce four full-color illustrations of scenes from the story, explaining why each would make a great cover for the book. You'll also write an interesting teaser for the back cover of the book, one that will hook readers into purchasing the book. Your final assignment is to create an exciting new book jacket that includes your favorite illustration for the cover, the writing for the back cover, and, of course, the book's title and author information.

Assignment

1. Select a challenging book to read for this project. Ask a language-arts teacher for recommendations, and be sure to get your supervising teacher's approval. Examine this assignment sheet carefully before you begin, so you understand the exact requirements. This will help you get ideas and make decisions about your project while you read your book.

2. Select at least four scenes from the book to illustrate. Choose scenes that will represent key points in the plot, important characters, or themes and that could represent the book as part of a book jacket design. Think about why you are choosing a particular scene to illustrate. You may use whatever medium you choose—for example, watercolor, marker, ink, collage, scratch board, or a combination of techniques—but each illustration must be full color and at least 8" x 10". (They may be larger if you wish.)

Check It Out

Society of Children's Book Writers and Illustrators

www.scbwi.org

SCBWI is the professional organization for people who write, illustrate, or share a vital interest in children's literature. The Web site offers information about the children's publishing industry and has links to other sites on writing and illustrating.

---

3. Write an appropriate caption for each illustration. The caption should tell what is happening in the scene, and it should be written as a part of the story. For example, for a scene from *The Hobbit* by J.R.R. Tolkien, a weak caption might be "This is Bilbo Baggins fighting the spiders." For a better caption, you might write "Nearly exhausted, brave little Bilbo fought with his tiny sword against the angry spiders."

4. Write a paragraph for each of your illustrations, explaining why you chose the scene and why the illustration would be suitable for a book cover. How would it interest readers? What elements of the story does it portray? Why do you like it?

5. Write enticing copy for the back of the book jacket. Think about the audience for your book. What readers are you trying to reach with the cover? Look at books you've chosen to read because of the cover copy; try to use similar techniques as you write the cover text for this book. The goal is to arouse the reader's curiosity, to give glimpses of the story without giving too many details, and to compel someone to take this book home and curl up on the sofa with it.

6. Design and create a jacket for the book. Select your favorite illustration for the front cover and incorporate your writing on the back of the jacket. Be sure to include the book's title, author, and illustrator in your cover design. Again, keep your audience in mind and look at other book covers to help you make decisions about how to style the title and the author and illustrator names. Make your book jacket large enough so that you have plenty of room to include everything.

7. (Optional) Many book covers rely on endorsements from respected experts or excerpts from reviews to help convince readers that the book is good. They usually take the form of several brief sentences or positive phrases on the back of the jacket or on the inside front flap of the book ("A deeply moving novel," or "Spellbinding!" or "The author takes you on a rollercoaster ride of adventures.") These comments, or testimonials, advertise the book's strengths. You may write your own comments or collect testimonials from friends who've read the book. Look over some published book jackets to get ideas about how this is done. You may also include a brief "About the Author" for the inside of the back cover of the jacket.

8. Organize and present your materials. You may choose to create a portfolio to present to the editor, or display them on a wall or table-top. Be prepared to answer questions and explain your work.

Notes

_____

_____

_____

_____

_____

_____

_____

_____

_____

_____

_____

_____

_____

_____

_____

_____

_____

_____

_____

_____

_____

_____

_____

Let Me Illustrate

A S S E S S M E N T   F O R M

STUDENT NAME

Student Responsibilities

- Read a challenging book.
- Identify four scenes from the story and illustrate them in great detail.
- Write a caption for each illustration, using an interesting narrative style.
- Explain the significance of each illustration.
- Write copy for the back cover of the book to introduce the book to readers.
- Design and create a book jacket.
- Produce a portfolio that contains all of the materials you created.
- Present the finished project.

ASSESSMENT SCALE
4 Exceeded Expectations
3 Achieved Expectations
2 Needs Time to Achieve Expectations
1 Showed Little or No Evidence that Expectations were Achieved

	SELF	TEACHER	OTHER
PROCESS			
1. Selected and read a challenging book.			
2. Selected four scenes to illustrate.			
3. Explained why each scene is significant.			
4. Applied writing skills to express ideas.			
5. Applied art skills to express ideas.			
6. Demonstrated creative-thinking skills.			
7. Combined project elements into a final product.			
8. Completed tasks in a timely manner.			
9. Solved problems independently.			
10. Presented information effectively.			
PRODUCTS			
11. Created three illustrations for the story.			
12. Created one illustration for the book jacket.			
13. Wrote an appropriate caption for each illustration.			
14. Provided a written explanation of why each illustration was chosen.			
15. Wrote copy for the back cover of the book.			
16. Designed an attractive book jacket.			
17. Organized the materials into a portfolio.			
18. Optional: Wrote testimonials for the book jacket.			
19. Optional: Wrote an "About the Author" paragraph.			
20.			
CONTENT			
21. Read a book as the basis for the project. Title: _____			
22. Interpreted four scenes from the story visually.			
23. Interpreted four scenes in writing.			
24. Explained the significance of each illustration.			
25. Introduced the book creatively.			
26.			
27.			
28.			
29.			
30.			

What's My Line?

Career Exploration

Many people don't think seriously about careers until they are forced to, but it's more fun to explore different possibilities when you have no pressure and a lot of time to think about it. There are thousands of career choices you might make, but opportunities don't show up on your doorstep; you need to seek them out. How do you know what the right career might be for you? How do you find out about what's even possible—or will be possible—in this fast-changing world? It's never too early to begin exploring your skills and interests and how they might translate into a rewarding career.

The scenario for this project is not imaginary. Every student in the world eventually participates in this scenario: Your task is to investigate an occupation to find out what it's all about. What does a person in this field do? What skills are needed? What type of education is required? What kinds of opportunities does the future hold? How might a student begin preparing for this career? What entry-level jobs exist, and how does someone advance? What kind of salary and other benefits can people in this career expect? The purpose of the project is for you to learn more about a specific career and to explain how a student might pursue it.

Project Scenario

You are a young adult who is trying to determine what to do after you graduate. After checking into a number of possibilities, you choose one career to learn more about. You'll do research to answer questions about necessary aptitudes and skills, specialty areas, related careers, formal education or vocational training requirements, salary ranges, and specific schools or colleges where you could become qualified for this job. Use your research to put together a packet of information about the career you studied and, finally, present what you learned to your classmates.

Assignment

1. Select a career to study. The form on page 103 will help you get started, or check out some of the interest self-tests at the Student Center Online (See Check It Out on page 102.) Once you've narrowed your options, write a description of the field that interests you and list possible jobs within that field. Find answers to the following questions:

- What skills should people in this field have?

- Are there specialty areas within the field?

- How do people in this field work with people in other fields?

- What related careers are possible for someone trained in this field?

- Are there professional organizations that help support people in this field?

- What salary and benefits can people in this career expect?

Give examples of typical jobs that someone in this field might perform. Tell why there is a continuing need for people to go into this career.

2. Interview at least two people who currently work in the occupation you are studying. (Be sure to get approval from your supervising teacher and parent or guardian.) Develop a list of interview questions that will help students (1) know what is involved in the day-to-day activities on the job, (2) decide if they might be interested in this line of work, and (3) think seriously about ways to prepare for this career. You may conduct the interviews in person, over the telephone, by letter, or through e-mail. (For interviewing tips, see page 135.) Write a summary of the interviews that will offer insight and advice to students from professionals in the field. Be sure to identify the people you interviewed. Send them copies of your summary and ask for their comments.

Finding People to Interview

How do you find people to interview? A good place to start is by talking to friends and family members or school guidance counselors—they might know someone who works in the field you're interested in. You can also check your local Yellow Pages for businesses in the categories that interest you. Call and ask if someone there would have time to talk to a student interested in that field. And ask the contacts you make for other contacts who might be willing to talk with you. If you're studying a career that has no representative in your area, do an Internet search or send letters or e-mail to professional organizations, employment agencies, postsecondary career placement offices, businesses, or agencies asking for help with your project.

3. Design a "map" that shows possible paths a student might follow to open the door to the career.

- Meet with a guidance counselor and discuss the high school curriculum that students interested in this career would likely follow.

- Does the job require training after high school? Find the course requirements and costs of at least three colleges or technical or trade schools that prepare students for this career. Select at least one out-of-state institution. Send letters to each institution you've identified asking for tuition costs, housing costs, and course requirements for the necessary degree or certification.

- Are internships, apprenticeships, or similar work-related experience recommended or required?

The first part of the map you create should include a path through the high school you will attend. Identify each semester and list the courses in which a student would probably enroll.

At the point of graduation from high school, divide the path into at least three different trails that represent possible paths to the career destination. Does this career require a college degree? Is there a specific curriculum that you must follow in college or can you choose among several different majors to reach the same goal? Can you start out by pursuing a technical curriculum or apprenticeship? Can you begin work directly in an entry-level position and get on-the-job training? Are there ways to combine education and experience, such as internships or military service? Include as much information as possible on your map: course titles, costs, time requirements, necessary degrees, possible side trails that students could follow.

End each trail at a door that opens to the career you've chosen.

4. Create a two-page overview of the career you studied. Present what you consider to be some of the most important facts and pieces of advice from your research. Your information will have to be concise and clearly outlined so that it allows someone to read it and quickly gain a basic understanding of the career and the qualifications a person needs to enter this field.

5. Present your project to your classmates.

Check It Out

100 Best Careers for the 21st Century by Shelly Field (New York: Macmillan, 1996). Written for young people preparing for a career, this book lists an expert's predictions on job opportunities in fast-growing career areas.

Career Paths
www.ipl.org/div/pathways
This site maintained by the Internet Public Library helps teens explore career choices, offers professional insight into individual careers, and provides tips on interviewing, cover letters, and résumés.

Cool Women, Hot Jobs . . . and how you can go for it, too! by Tina Schwager, P.T.A., A.T.,C., and Michele Schuerger (Minneapolis: Free Spirit Publishing, 2002). Women's career options used to be limited, but not anymore. In this book, twenty-two women tell about their work, how they got started, what they do, and why they love it.

Quintessential Careers
www.quintcareers.com/teens.html
This collection of career information and job-hunting resources has links to a wide range of sites that offer job listings, career exploration, assessments, and more.

What's My Line?

GETTING STARTED

Use this form to help you think about the career area you may like to study. Each item is just a starting point since there may be hundreds of different jobs available in that field of work. Feel free to add career areas that are not on this list.

1. Put an *x* in front of the fields that interest you the most.

__ accounting	__ customer service	__ health	__ plumbing
__ aeronautics	__ dance	__ history	__ politics
__ agriculture	__ dentistry	__ home business	__ public relations
__ architecture	__ detective work	__ home economics	__ publishing
__ art	__ driver	__ horticulture	__ research
__ automotives	__ education/teaching	__ hospitality	__ retail
__ banking	__ electrical	__ investment	__ robotics
__ beauty	__ engineering	__ journalism	__ sales
__ biology	__ entertainment	__ judicial system	__ science
__ business	__ environment	__ landscaping	__ social work
__ charity organizations	__ factory work	__ law	__ stock market
__ child care	__ fitness	__ law enforcement	__ systems
__ clothing/fashion	__ foreign policy	__ machinery	__ tourism
__ computers	__ gardening	__ management	__ trade jobs
__ construction	__ genetics	__ math	__ training animals
__ consulting	__ geography	__ medicine	__ transportation
__ cooking	__ geology	__ music	__ waste management
__ cultural studies	__ geriatrics	__ office work	__ weather
__ current events	__ government	__ parenting	__ writing

2. Look at the items you checked, and list the three general areas that interest you the most. If you're interested in something that is not on the list, write it in.

_____   _____   _____

3. After looking over preliminary information about your three interest areas, choose one to study for this project: _____

4. As you do research, list specific careers that relate to the field you are studying.

_____   _____   _____

_____   _____   _____

Note: Even though you aren't required to keep a portfolio for this project, you can start putting one together now to help you explore educational and career choices in the future. Start a file folder (or folders) where you can store examples of your best work and documentation of your achievements in school and your community. As you add to the file throughout the years, you will be compiling evidence of your interest areas and abilities. More and more schools require students to make portfolios, which can be used to show prospective schools or employers what skills and experience you have to offer.

What's My Line?

ASSESSMENT FORM

STUDENT NAME

Student Responsibilities

- Select a career to study and explain what someone in that field might do.
- Identify two professionals in the career, interview them, and write a summary.
- Meet with a guidance counselor to determine a likely high school curriculum for students interested in pursuing this career.
- Contact three postsecondary institutions to determine how to obtain a degree or training that could lead to employment in this career (get costs and coursework).
- Develop a "map" that shows possible paths from ninth grade to a job in this career.
- Present the finished project.
- Demonstrate knowledge of the career by answering reasonable questions.

ASSESSMENT SCALE

4 Exceeded Expectations

3 Achieved Expectations

2 Needs Time to Achieve Expectations

1 Showed Little or No Evidence that Expectations were Achieved

	SELF	TEACHER	OTHER
PROCESS			
1. Chose an appropriate career to study.			
2. Applied interviewing skills.			
3. Applied letter-writing skills.			
4. Applied research skills to find information and cited sources.			
5. Applied writing skills to express ideas.			
6. Expressed ideas visually.			
7. Demonstrated creative thinking skills.			
8. Completed tasks in a timely manner.			
9. Solved problems independently.			
10. Presented information effectively.			
PRODUCTS			
11. Composed an explanation of a career.			
12. Conducted at least two interviews.			
13. Wrote a summary of the two interviews.			
14. Wrote letters to at least three schools.			
15. Discussed high school courses with a counselor.			
16. Designed and produced a "career map."			
17. Created a two-page overview of a career.			
18.			
19.			
20.			
CONTENT			
21. Described the form and function of a career.			
22. Analyzed educational and training requirements for a career.			
23. Identified possible paths to the career.			
24. Determined the cost of becoming a professional in the chosen career.			
25. Developed key questions for interviews and/or letters.			
26. Gave informed answers to questions.			
27.			
28.			
29.			
30.			

May I Help You?

Service Learning

Service learning offers you an opportunity to become involved in your community as part of your school experience. Service-learning students take part in a wide range of community projects—everything from helping in their neighborhood, to cleaning up a lakeshore, to carrying out experiments for a scientific organization. Service learning is designed to let students connect their education with real-world experiences. And students not only learn about their communities, but the communities also benefit from the service that students provide.

Do you have an interest area that you care deeply about, such as the environment or homelessness or human rights? Are you looking for an opportunity to make a difference in your community by helping at a food bank, monitoring contaminants in streams or lakes, or teaching kids to read? Is there a service organization that could help you explore career goals as you help them in some way?

Service learning lets you learn practical skills for life and work. You will gain new knowledge, valuable experience, and insight as you give something back to the community.

This project will help you make the connection between school and community through a service-learning experience. It asks you to identify three needs or problems in your local community and choose one to focus on. You will create a plan for becoming involved with a local organization, complete the service work, and keep a journal to record what you learned through your service.

Project Scenario

You participate in your school's service-learning program, and your advisor has asked you to help show younger students and community members how kids at your school are working to make a difference in the local community. You want to encourage others to participate, and you've been asked to include excerpts from your service-learning journal and photos that show some of your service activities.

Assignment

1. Begin a service-learning journal. Use it as a place to record your research, plans, experiences, feelings, and the results of the service project you design. Be sure to write in your journal at every step of your project so you have a complete record of your experience.

2. Conduct a needs-assessment of your community (your school, neighborhood, or town). Discuss your project with friends, neighbors, classmates, teachers, parents, and other community members. Tell them you are compiling a list of needs or problems that students your age might be able to do something about. Keep a running record of your list in your journal. For example:

- Some children aren't being read to as much as they would like.

- The area around our school looks trashy.

- Many residents in the nursing home down the street are lonely.

Look for issues or problems that you feel are important. What things could be improved in the neighborhood or community—and what would it take to help? What can you learn by working with this issue? How can it fit with your school goals?

> ### Check It Out
>
> ***The Kid's Guide to Service Projects: Over 500 Service Ideas for Young People Who Want to Make a Difference*** by Barbara A. Lewis (Minneapolis: Free Spirit Publishing, 1995). Hundreds of ideas for all kinds of service projects, from simple ones anyone can do to large-scale commitments that involve whole communities.
>
> ***The Kid's Guide to Social Action: How to Solve the Social Problems You Choose—And Turn Creative Thinking into Positive Action*** by Barbara A. Lewis (Minneapolis: Free Spirit Publishing, 1998). Filled with real stories about real kids who have made a difference in their world, this practical guide offers step-by-step help in writing letters, interviewing, making speeches, fundraising, getting media coverage and more.
>
> **The National Youth Leadership Council**
> *www.nylc.org*
> Works to encourage youth leadership and service learning; sponsors conferences, a magazine, books, videos, and a clearinghouse for service.

3. After you have compiled a list with many options, choose at least three specific local needs that interest you and look like real possibilities for a service learning project. In your journal, describe these three needs more fully and suggest ideas for getting involved. Produce a two-column chart. Label the first column "Needs in Our Community"; call the second column "How Students Can Help." In the first column, list the three needs that you have identified, and in the second, record ideas of how students can help. Your chart should show at least one way that students can help meet each need. Record your drafts and your final chart in your journal.

4. Choose one of the three needs that most interests you and where you feel you'd like to invest your energies. Begin a personal plan for becoming involved in implementing a solution. This will take some careful consideration. Ask yourself, What can I realistically do? What time constraints do I have? What kind of a commitment does this project involve? What are the potential benefits of this option? In what ways can I have a positive impact on this problem? How can I connect this service to my classes at school?

5. Outline the plan carefully and completely in your journal. The plan should:

- Identify organizations in your community that can help you fill the needs you identified.

- Identify at least two adults who could help you create a plan and coordinate your activities. (This should include at least one parent or guardian, and perhaps a teacher or a volunteer coordinator at a local organization.)

- Make arrangements with one of your teachers to present your work to a class, to show how service learning is connected to school learning.

- With the support of the adults you've chosen to help you get started, describe the tasks you will perform.

- Explain in detail what you expect to accomplish by performing these tasks: What results are you looking for?

- Establish a schedule that specifies where you will perform the service and the amount of time you will devote to it each week.

Try to include as much information as possible in your journal as you are developing your plan.

6. Carry out your service-learning activity. Be sure to keep journal notes as well as other records, including photographs or videotape documenting your work, any posters, flyers, or other material you create, comments from people you worked with.

7. Prepare a visual display of your activities; for example:

- Mount your photographs on posterboard with captions that explain what the pictures show.

- Narrate a videotape that describes what is being shown.

8. As your project wraps up, write about your accomplishments, insights, feelings, and disappointments in the journal. The final journal entry should carefully assess how successful your efforts were. Did you achieve the expected results? Your honest assessment of what didn't work very well is also important. Some of the most valuable learning comes from reflecting on how you might have improved your success by doing things differently.

9. Present your work to other students, emphasizing your project and how what you learned through service can be directly connected to what you learn through school.

10. Present your work to parents or community members.

May I Help You?
A S S E S S M E N T F O R M

Student Responsibilities

- Detail the service-learning experience in a journal.
- Determine what needs in your community you might address.
- Describe three local needs as fully and accurately as possible.
- Produce a chart listing possible student-based solutions to the needs you identify.
- Create a plan for helping solve one of the needs.
- Carry out your service-learning plan.
- Document the experience through journal writing and photographs or video.
- Present your finished project to a class and to another audience.

<table>
<tr><th colspan="2">ASSESSMENT SCALE</th></tr>
<tr><td>4</td><td>Exceeded Expectations</td></tr>
<tr><td>3</td><td>Achieved Expectations</td></tr>
<tr><td>2</td><td>Needs Time to Achieve Expectations</td></tr>
<tr><td>1</td><td>Showed Little or No Evidence that Expectations were Achieved</td></tr>
</table>

	SELF	TEACHER	OTHER
PROCESS			
1. Assessed the needs in the community.			
2. Interviewed people in the community for input about needs.			
3. Analyzed three needs to determine what can be done.			
4. Identified one need to work on.			
5. Performed a service-learning activity.			
6. Analyzed the results of the activity (your degree of success).			
7. Applied photography or video skills.			
8. Applied best writing skills.			
9. Applied problem-solving strategies.			
10. Presented information effectively.			
PRODUCTS			
11. Produced a journal to document the service learning experience.			
12. Recorded three carefully written local needs.			
13. Produced a chart showing three needs and ways to help.			
14. Created a plan for becoming involved with one need.			
15. Identified organizations that address the selected need.			
16. Identified two adults to help coordinate activities.			
17. Described tasks to be performed.			
18. Established a schedule for performing the service.			
19. Documented the experience with photos or on videotape.			
20.			
CONTENT			
21. Discovered local needs and problems.			
22. Developed possible solutions to local needs and problems.			
23. Solicited the opinions of community members.			
24. Recorded the results of personal effort and involvement.			
25. Made specific connections between your service and school learning.			
26.			
27.			
28.			
29.			
30.			

Student Mentor

Mentorship

This project is different from all the others in *Challenging Projects for Creative Minds*. It is a *mentor* project, which means that your primary responsibility is not to complete your own project, but to help other students plan and complete their projects. If you like working with other students, if you have tutoring experience, or if you are thinking about teaching as a profession, this is a good project for you.

To be eligible for this project you must have completed at least one project and received a Certificate of Merit in the past two years.

Project Scenario

You are a teaching assistant in your school. Your job is to help students complete individualized and small-group projects in an enrichment program. Students who need help come to you first, before going to the supervising teacher. You are skilled at helping students think through their problems and guiding them to come up with workable solutions on their own. You are also trained in information

management and presentation skills. Students look to you for advice on finding information, putting it into presentation form, and communicating it to others in a variety of ways.

Assignment

When you decide to become a student mentor, supervising teachers will count on you to help people without giving them the answers or doing the work for them. Students will count on you to be available to help them. You will gain a sense of accomplishment that comes from helping other students produce high-quality projects. The general responsibilities of a mentor are listed below. You will work directly with at least one supervising teacher to determine what your specific responsibilities will be.

1. Read each of the *Challenging Projects* to become familiar with the choices students will be making. One of your jobs will be to talk with students who are trying to decide which project to choose. You can be helpful by listening to students as they talk about various ideas, suggesting projects or options that they might find interesting, and then discussing the benefits and opportunities each has to offer.

2. Help students plan their projects once they are chosen. The projects require students to make many important decisions. For example, they may have to choose a topic, decide how they will present their information, select appropriate resources, identify potential audiences, and so forth. There are many suggestions and forms throughout this book that can help students with this part of a project.

Note: You should never do any work for students or try to simplify their task by offering absolute answers. Your job is to help them find their own answers by asking questions that will lead to workable solutions. This is not always easy, but with practice you can become good at it. For example, you might ask, What other ways can you look at this problem? What ideas do you have so far? What resources have you used and where else can you find information? Have you thought about how you'll organize your research? How are the plans for your presentation working out?

3. Offer suggestions to students who are working on their projects and need help. Once again, you can do this by asking questions so that the solutions and ideas are the students' and not yours: "Here's what worked for me when I did my project. Your audience is different, though, so what might you try instead?" But you may also need to point out options, offer differing viewpoints, and give helpful advice or moral support.

4. Keep a log book or journal to record each time you help a student. Describe what you did and comment on each student's progress (level of independence, commitment to quality, perseverance, creativity, problem-solving skills, forms or ideas that were helpful, and so forth). Journal entries provide valuable insight into the creative process, learning strategies, and student motivation, and they also become evidence of your level of involvement as a student mentor. Use your journal as a place for positive or constructive analysis of a student's progress. Record what students do well and the strengths that you observe. Don't look for faults, but try to help students strengthen their project and write about their work with respect.

5. Fill out the "Other" column on the Performance Assessment Form for students assigned to you by a supervising teacher. You are in a unique position to assess end results because you have watched the development of projects over a period of time. Expect high quality from students and be prepared to explain how quality could be improved. Write a brief summary of what the student achieved with the project and attach it to the assessment form.

6. Assist the supervising teachers in the day-to-day operation of the program. You may be asked to take attendance, check on resources, help make arrangements for exhibits, monitor daily progress, and so on.

7. Analyze and evaluate your mentor experience to identify ten tips for students who sign up for future projects. Use these tips to create a handout students could use next year.

8. Present your ten tips and other insights about successfully completing a project.

9. Ask your supervising teacher for help when necessary.

Student Mentor

A S S E S S M E N T   F O R M

STUDENT NAME

Student Responsibilities

- Assist students in selecting a project.
- Assist students in completing a project.
- Contribute to the program by helping teachers in a variety of ways.
- Produce a log or journal to record daily work, ideas, progress of students, etc.
- Provide a peer assessment for the final project of each assigned student.
- Create "Ten Tips for Success" based on what you've learned.
- Present your tips and other insights on doing a project.

<table>
<tr><td colspan="2">ASSESSMENT SCALE</td></tr>
<tr><td>4</td><td>Exceeded Expectations</td></tr>
<tr><td>3</td><td>Achieved Expectations</td></tr>
<tr><td>2</td><td>Needs Time to Achieve Expectations</td></tr>
<tr><td>1</td><td>Showed Little or No Evidence that Expectations were Achieved</td></tr>
</table>

		SELF	TEACHER	OTHER
PROCESS	1. Became familiar with available projects.			
	2. Provided help for students who needed it.			
	3. Applied writing skills to express ideas.			
	4. Demonstrated planning skills.			
	5. Demonstrated problem-solving skills.			
	6. Demonstrated research skills.			
	7. Demonstrated creative-thinking skills.			
	8. Demonstrated a commitment to quality.			
	9. Demonstrated personal responsibility.			
	10. Asked for help from a supervising teacher when appropriate.			
PRODUCTS	11. Produced a log book or journal.			
	12. Assisted students with presentation ideas.			
	13. Wrote ten tips for success.			
	14.			
	15.			
	16.			
	17.			
	18.			
	19.			
	20.			
CONTENT	21. Became familiar with the content requirements of all projects.			
	22. Recorded an assessment for each student supervised.			
	23. Advised students on topics and information management.			
	24. Provided positive and constructive feedback to students.			
	25. Summarized effective project strategies.			
	26.			
	27.			
	28.			
	29.			
	30.			

Design Your Own Project

Do you have an idea for a project that isn't in this book? You may prefer to work on your own idea because it interests you more than anything else right now. In this incredibly diverse world, no book can provide projects for every interest that students may have. So if you are willing to work with a teacher to write up your idea, you can create the project that is perfect for you.

The purpose of designing your own project is to allow you to pursue a personal interest area, not to teach you how to write curriculum. Students across the country have designed their own projects to fit their personal needs. Some students use an existing project as a template or model for a project on a different topic. One budding archeologist recreated "It's Written in the Stars" to become "It's Written in the Bones," and based his project on a study of fossils. Other students have created entirely new projects. Britt Cecconi of Stillwater, Minnesota, became a restaurant reviewer and self-published a book *& Pans: A Fourteen-Year-Old's Guide to Eating Out in the Twin Cities.* Do you have a strong interest you'd like to pursue? Here's an opportunity.

Writing Your Own Project

The project you create will be similar to those in this book. That means you'll set up the project within a **Scenario** that you invent, organize what you will do into **Assignment** steps, and create an **Assessment** form for your project. Here's an introduction to the process of writing a project. Specific steps you'll need to complete begin on page 114.

Writing the Scenario

Scenarios stage a lifelike role for you to play. If you're interested in health topics, for instance, your scenario could be that you are part of a rap group that has been hired by the American Lung Association to produce a videotape that teaches kids about the hazards of smoking. Maybe your interest lies in the preservation of the rain forest. Your scenario could have you working with a team of Brazilian scientists to create an exhibit that will travel to national museums to highlight the beauty and fragility of the rain forest.

Your scenario must describe four aspects of the project: (1) what **role** you play, (2) what your **assignment** is within that role, (3) what **products** you will create, and (4) what type of final **presentation** you will make. Remember: Your supervising teacher will work with you throughout the project writing process, so don't let all these instructions scare you.

Many, many different scenarios could be written for the exact same topic, so there is no one right or best scenario. Develop your scenario around your strengths and learning styles. If you are not musically inclined (like the rap project person would be) but are interested in doing a project on smoking, you could build your scenario around what you are already good at or something you would like to try. For example, look at the following possible scenarios for developing a project about smoking. They all involve different skills, background knowledge, activities, and interests. You could be a:

- Statistician who has been hired by the Health Department to produce charts and graphs that illustrate data related to smoking.

- Teacher who has been asked to produce a series of lessons about smoking for a new third-grade health book.

- Journalist who writes a feature article for the Sunday paper about smoking.

- Photographer who documents a day in the life of a heavy smoker.

- Artist who creates a poster for a "Celebrate Life Festival" that deglamorizes smoking and shows the benefits of not smoking.

- Prominent physician who does workshops to train future doctors about the diseases associated with smoking.

- Radio personality who invites a group of people to talk about smoking on the morning show.

Writing the Assignment

The next part of the project that you will write is the **Assignment**. Write the assignment in numbered steps that tell what you will do, what you will produce, and what you will present. If you are part of the rap group whose job it is to produce a video about smoking, a brief version of your assignment might look like this example:

For this project I will:

1. Contact the American Lung Association for information about the health risks of smoking and find at least two other sources of information about the health problems that can result from smoking or breathing secondhand smoke.

2. Find information about why people start to smoke, at what age people typically start to smoke, and how much it costs to smoke.

3. Write a rap that could be used on TV as a public service announcement to alert young people to the dark side of smoking.

4. Plan ways to make the rap interesting and visually effective.

5. Arrange to have my rap taped after I have practiced it thoroughly.

6. Videotape my rap performance.

7. Design an attractive, informative poster to go with the video. On the poster, I will include some background information about myself, a brief essay that explains my views on why smoking should get a bad rap, and some type of graphic that will attract people's attention. I will also add other things that might make the poster more effective or interesting.

8. Show the tape to an audience and answer any questions the audience may have.

Writing the Assessment Form

The third part of the project is the **Assessment** form. You may develop an assessment with the help of your supervising teacher or use the one provided with this project. This form will guide you in meeting the project requirements you design and help you assess how well you've achieved what you set out to do.

Before You Begin

Before you actually begin writing the project, meet with a supervising teacher to discuss your plan and get any necessary information and forms. Once you have a basic idea of what it takes to write your own project, look over some of the projects in this book to see how they are organized and written. Be sure to discuss the project with friends, parents, or others who can help you organize and describe it. The guidelines on the following pages will help you create an interesting and workable design.

Forms to help you write your own project:

- Narrowing the Topic (see page 126)
- Introduction & Scenario (see page 141)
  Use the Scenario portion.
- Assignment Form (see page 142)
- Assessment Form (see page 143)
- Project Request Form (see page 120)
- Strategy Sheet (see pages 127–128)

Assignment

1. Choose a topic to study. The purpose of these projects is to provide opportunities for you to learn about things that you find personally interesting. Since you will spend a lot of time studying the topic you choose, make sure it is something you want to learn about. You can choose a fairly broad topic at this point, but you will need to narrow it down as you decide on the details of your project.

Defining a Topic

For your final project you'll need to narrow your ideas down to one specific, workable topic. For example, don't choose to study "animals"—that is much too general. You couldn't possibly design a project that would cover the topic adequately. Narrow your focus to something that can be covered in a single project, such as penguins or animal life in a freshwater pond or training dogs to rescue people buried in avalanches or collapsed buildings. Ancient civilizations is another topic that would take years to study. Even selecting one ancient civilization such as the Mayans or the Shang dynasty in China can be too broad. You could narrow your focus to "What the Nile River meant to ancient Egypt" or "Architecture of ancient Greece" or "How archeology has helped us learn about ancient civilizations." No matter what you decide to study, be sure to focus your topic on something very specific. (See page 126 for help in narrowing your topic.)

2. Compose a first draft Scenario for the project you are proposing (see page 141). The project scenario is like a brief story that sets the stage for the assignment. It provides a role for you to play as you complete the project. It also gives general guidelines for the products or artifacts that you will create and the presentation you will give. The scenario you write can be completely imaginary, or it can be based in reality. For example, you might create a scenario in which you are a space explorer who visits a distant planet to collect information for a national space museum. Or you might be a landscaper who's been hired to create a hedge maze at a country estate. Examine the scenarios from other projects in this book to see how they are written. Model your writing after these examples.

3. Write your Project Assignment (see page 152). List each step to provide a clear picture of what you will do to complete the project. Since the steps and activities are entirely up to you, think through the assignment carefully. List everything you can think of that you will have to do to finish the project. You can't have too many steps! The more detailed you are, the better. Spend some time on this. When you've listed all the steps you can think of, number the items in the order that they must be done. (Number 1 is the first thing you will do, then number 2, and so on.) Examine the project assignments from the projects in this book to see how they are written. Model your writing after these examples.

Keep in mind that you must end up with at least one product (something that you have produced) that can be displayed or presented to other people. You may have had a specific presentation in mind when you chose your topic or wrote your scenario. Or your topic may suggest a certain type of presentation. For example, if your topic is woodworking, or cooking, or genealogy, the products that you might produce lend themselves to specific kinds of presentations—a completed carpentry project, a meal, a family tree.

4. Use the Project Request Form (see page 120) to submit your proposed project for approval. Below is a list of things that must be included for your idea to be accepted:

a) On the line labeled "Title of New Project," write "Design Your Own Project." This will tell the supervising teacher that you are requesting

Presenting Your Project

Here are some ideas for presenting your project. Be sure to determine who the audience will be.

- Oral presentation to the class or a team of teachers
- Display somewhere in the school building (posters, bulletin boards, models, dioramas, exhibits, demonstrations, and so forth)
- Display in a public building (library, administration office, nature center, museum, government office, and so forth)
- Video or audio presentation
- Written report, story, or poem, perhaps with illustrations, for display in the media center or elementary buildings
- A presentation or lesson to children at an elementary school
- Computer presentation or Web site
- Dramatic, musical, or artistic concert, recital, or performance
- Speech to an audience (student assembly, staff meeting, community group, and so forth)
- Special display at parent conferences

to work on a project of your own design.

b) On the next line, describe the specific topic you wish to study.

c) Attach the Project Scenario and Assignment that you've written. This will give the supervising teacher a clear idea of what you intend to do.

d) Complete the rest of the Project Request Form and any other forms your teacher gave you and turn them in for approval.

5. Once your project has been approved, you'll meet with your supervising teacher to receive a Project Packet and to go over the assessment form.

6. Fill out a Project Strategy Sheet (See pages 127–128).

7. Work to complete your project and present it.

Design Your Own Project

ASSESSMENT FORM

STUDENT NAME

Student Responsibilities

- Choose a topic of interest.
- Write a scenario describing an imaginary situation that requires a presentation.
- Decide on a set of artifacts to produce for display (to show what has been learned).
- Identify a method of presenting the finished project publicly.
- Produce a written assignment based on the format used in other projects.
- Develop a plan that specifies how the project will be conducted.
- Complete and present the project to an audience.

ASSESSMENT SCALE

4 Exceeded Expectations

3 Achieved Expectations

2 Needs Time to Achieve Expectations

1 Showed Little or No Evidence that Expectations were Achieved

	SELF	TEACHER	OTHER
PROCESS			
1. Chose a topic of personal interest to study.			
2. Demonstrated creative-thinking skills.			
3. Invented a project scenario.			
4. Identified a role to play within the scenario.			
5. Developed a plan for completing the project.			
6. Developed a plan for presenting the project.			
7. Followed plans well; changed plans when necessary.			
8. Applied necessary skills (e.g., writing, art, research).			
9. Solved problems independently.			
10. Presented information effectively.			
PRODUCTS			
11. Composed a project scenario.			
12. Produced a written assignment with each step listed.			
13. Completed a Project Request Form and a Strategy Sheet.			
14. Produced these products:			
15.			
16.			
17.			
18.			
19.			
20.			
CONTENT			
21. Studied this topic: _____.			
22. Located important or pertinent information.			
23. Demonstrated knowledge of the topic.			
24. Explained the topic in an understandable way.			
25. Gave informed answers to reasonable questions.			
26.			
27.			
28.			
29.			
30.			

Project Forms
and Resources

Forms for Students

Project Request Form

Name: _____ Date: _____

Grade: _____ Team: _____

If this is a group project, list the other members of your group. (Note: Each student in the group must fill out a separate form, and all forms must be turned in together.)

Please answer the following questions:

1. Are you currently passing all of your classes in school? ☐ Yes ☐ No

2. Have you worked on a project before? ☐ Yes ☐ No

3. If yes, what was the title of the project you did? _____

4. If yes, did you receive a certificate for it? ☐ Yes ☐ No

5. Title of new project: _____

6. Briefly explain why you want to do this project. _____

_____

_____

_____

_____

_____

I want to work on a Creative Minds project. I understand that to earn a certificate I must follow the project assignment and make a commitment to do my very best work. I accept that responsibility. I will conduct my project under the guidance of a supervising teacher, who will meet with me as needed to discuss my progress and final presentation.

Student signature: _____ Date: _____

I have read the Creative Minds project that my child has chosen. I have also discussed the project requirements with my child. I agree to support my child's work and monitor my child's progress during the course of the project.

Parent or guardian signature: _____ Date: _____

Permission is granted for the student named above to begin work on the Creative Minds project described on this form.

Supervising teacher signature: _____ Date: _____

Group Discussion Checklist

STUDENT NAME _____

Project title: _____   Supervising teacher: _____

At least one group member should take notes during the discussion. Everyone should have a copy of the project description for reference.

☐ Read and discuss the project scenario.

☐ List the products the assignment asks us to produce (for example, chart, poster, brochure).

☐ List the tasks we have to do for the project (for example, keep a journal, conduct a poll, work in the community, practice a performance).

☐ Brainstorm ideas for creating the final presentation.

☐ Determine what parts of the project require research. What do we already know? What do we need to find out?

☐ What resources are available to help us with our research?

At school	At home	In the community	Other
books	technology	local experts	_____
technology	books	businesses	_____
Internet	family members	museums/libraries	_____
teachers	neighbors	organizations	_____
librarians		colleges	_____

☐ Decide who will be responsible for each task. What parts of the project is each group member interested in doing? (See Group Project Planner, page 122.)

☐ Develop a time line for the project. Discuss times and due dates so everyone knows what should be done by the next meeting. When is the next meeting? When is the Midproject Report due?

☐ Discuss how the project will be assessed. Go over the assessment form in the Project Packet, and discuss with the supervising teacher how it applies to the group.

☐ List the materials we need to do the project. Where can we find these materials? What costs are involved? Who is responsible for getting the materials?

☐ What other questions do we have?

Group Project Planner

Project title: _____   Supervising teacher: _____

List the group members in the first column. Refer to the Project Assignment as you discuss and decide what tasks need to be done to complete the project. Write these tasks across the top row. As a group, decide who will do what for each task. You may need to use several sheets.

GROUP MEMBERS	TASK # ____	TASK # ____	TASK # ____	TASK # ____
1.				
2.				
3.				
4.				
5.				

Sample Group Project Planner

Project title: __Great Performances__

Supervising teacher: __Mrs. Holts__

List the group members in the first column. Refer to the Project Assignment as you discuss and decide what tasks need to be done to complete the project. Write these tasks across the top row. As a group, decide who will do what for each task. You may need to use several sheets.

GROUP MEMBERS	TASK # 1 Design a poster to advertise program.	TASK # 2 Compose a program guide.	TASK # 3 Set up schedules, videotaping, props.	TASK # 4 Present the program.
1. Mark	- Write text for the poster. - Help Marissa make posters.	Write bio for program guide.		Play saxophone (accompanied by piano)
2. Alicia	Help J.Q. put posters up.	- Help J.Q. with program guide. - Write bio.		Juggling and magic show
3. Marissa	- Design the artwork. - Produce 3 posters.	Write bio.		-Jazz -Dance
4. J.Q.	Help Alicia put posters up.	Design and assemble program guide.	-Reserve room. -Arrange videotaping. -Set up group meetings. -Track project/timeline.	-Pass out programs. -Announce performances. -Help with videotaping.
5.				

From *Challenging Projects for Creative Minds* by Phil Schlemmer, M.Ed., and Dori Schlemmer © 1999. Free Spirit Publishing Inc.. Minneapolis, MN; 800/735-7323; www.freespirit.com. This page may be photocopied for individual, classroom, or group work only.

Detailed Student Planner

STUDENT NAME

Project title: _____ Supervising teacher: _____

Use this form to detail what you will do for each task you are responsible for.
Use more forms if needed.

Important Dates

Midproject Report: _____

Performance: _____

TASK

To do:

TASK

To do:

TASK

To do:

Sample Detailed Student Planner

Project title: __Great Performances__

Student name: __Mark__

Supervising teacher: __Mrs. Holts__

Important Dates

Midproject Report: __Jan. 20__

Performance: __March 27__

Use this form to detail what you will do for each task you are responsible for. Use more forms if needed.

TASK

Write text for the poster.

To do:

- Meet with Marissa to brainstorm ideas for poster.

- Set up time to word process in the computer lab.

- Get performance site and time from J.Q.

- Have draft text done by Dec. 2 (group meeting)

TASK

Write biography for program.

To do:

- Talk with group about format/style of bio. (1st or 3rd person)

- Write my biography for program guide. Have Dad read it over.

- Give bio. to J.Q. at group meeting Jan. 8

TASK

Play saxophone at performance.

To do:

- Ask band director for music suggestions.

- Set up practice times with pianist (Joel)

- Practice before school M,T,Th.

- Play pieces for band director end of Jan. to get feedback.

- Polish saxophone on March 26.

Narrowing the Topic

STUDENT NAME

Almost everyone will tell you, deciding on a topic can be the most difficult choice you make when beginning a project. Let's say you want to learn more about music. That's a good place to start, but you have a lot of thinking and some research to do before you can narrow that down to a manageable size. Do you want to study classical, jazz, or pop? A specific musician or a musical era? The music of Africa, the Andes, or the United States? Or are you more interested in performing or learning a new technique or studying what jobs are available in the music industry?

Use this form as you begin your research to help you zero in on what you will study. You may hit upon the perfect topic right away as you find fasci-

nating resources on a subject you already know something about. Or you might take some time browsing through resources and talking to people to discover topics you know little about. However you approach it, narrowing your topic to something specific lets you create a richer and more interesting project.

1. What general category are you interested in?

2. What are more specific topics in that category?

3. Begin your research to find out more specific subtopics for each topic above.

4. Look over your subtopics and choose one, or look for a theme that could be the focus of your project.

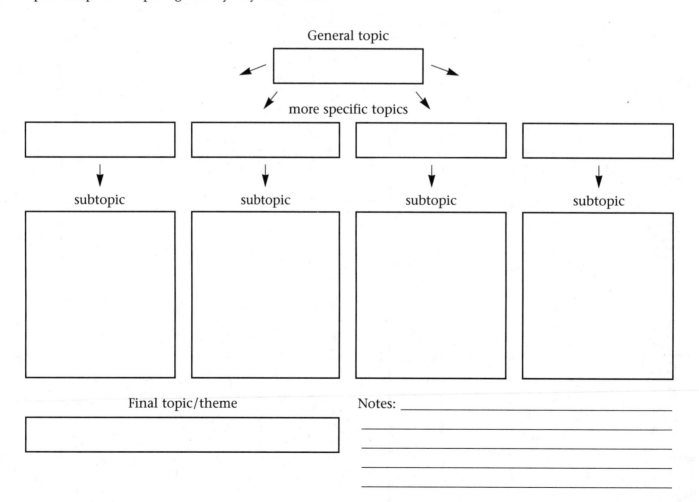

 # Strategy Sheet

STUDENT NAME

Project title: _____ Date: _____

Getting Started

Briefly describe the topic of your project. What specifically are you going to study?

_____

_____

_____

When will you work on the project?

_____

_____

Finding Information

What parts of the project require research? What information do you need? What questions will help you guide your research?

_____

_____

_____

_____

What resources can you use to find information about the topic you are studying (books, magazines, people, Web sites, organizations, colleges)? List possible resources below:

1. _____

2. _____

3. _____

4. _____

5. _____

6. _____

continued on next page. . .

Presentation

A major requirement of these projects is that you must present work publicly. How will you present your finished project to other people? Talk to your teachers about some suggestions if you have trouble with this section. List two ideas for presenting your project:

1. _____

2. _____

What materials do you need for your project, and where can you find them?

_____

_____

_____

_____

_____

_____

Outline the major steps of your project and tell what you plan to do to complete each part of the assignment. When you've listed all the steps you can think of, number the steps to prioritize your tasks. What is the first thing you will need to do? What should you do next? (Use another sheet of paper.)

Progress Report

Midway through the project you will formally report on your progress to your supervising teacher. Select a meeting date that will give you enough time to get a good start on the project.

Midproject Report due _____.

Due Date

I will turn in my completed project to my supervising teacher on _____.

List of Resources

Use this sheet to record detailed information for each resource that you use in your project. This list will help you give credit to your sources, locate the information again, and help others who do similar research find useful information.

Many books are available on creating a bibliography and citing sources (see your language-arts textbook, or ask a teacher for help). Here are some basic examples that you can follow to be sure that you include all important information about each source you use:

Book

- Author's name (last name first)
- Title of book (in italics or underlined)
- City of publication
- Publisher
- Copyright date
- The pages you used in your research

Example:

Greenfield, Susan A. *The Human Brain,* New York: BasicBooks, 1997. Page 160.

Magazine or Newspaper Article

- Author's name (last name first)
- Title of article (in quotation marks)
- Title of publication (in italics or underlined)
- Date and year of publication
- The pages you used in your research

Example:

Begley, Sharon. "Memories are made of...," *Newsweek,* November 4, 1996. Page 68.

Interview

- Name of person interviewed (last name first)
- Name of interviewer
- Type of interview conducted (for example, tape recording, video recording, online interview)
- Place of interview
- Date of interview

Example:

Leitz, Scott. Interview by Autumn Mitchell. Tape recording. Chicago, IL. June 10, 1998.

Film or Video

- Title of film or video (in italics or underlined)
- Date (if available)
- Other information that would help the reader

Example:

The Magnificent Brain, 1998. Video produced by EVC Productions, New York City.

Internet Site

- Author's name (last name first), if available
- Title of article or feature (in quotation marks)
- Title of Web magazine or Web site (in italics or underlined)
- Web site address
- Date the information was posted (if available)

Example:

Chudler, Eric. "Brain Development," *Neuroscience for Kids,* faculty.washington.edu/chudler/dev.html June 17, 1998.

continued on next page. . .

Author	Title	Other information	Date	Page numbers

Project Log

Project title: _____

Use this log to keep an accurate and complete record of your work.

DATE	TIME SPENT	WORK DONE

continued on next page. . .

PROJECT LOG CONTINUED. . .

DATE	TIME SPENT	WORK DONE

I hereby verify that, to the best of my knowledge, my child, _____, did the work listed above and the time recorded is an accurate account of the time actually invested in the project.

Parent or guardian signature: _____ Date: _____

Midproject Report Form

STUDENT NAME _____

Project title: _____   Date: _____

1. What progress are you making on your project?

☐ Things are going well.
☐ I've run into a few problems.
☐ I'm really stuck!

What's going particularly well? What problems have you encountered?

_____

_____

_____

2. Are you following the requirements on your Project Assignment Sheet and the plan on your Strategy Sheet?

☐ Yes, very closely.
☐ I've had to make some changes.
☐ The plan isn't working!

Here's what I need to change:

_____

_____

_____

3. How much time have you spent working on your project? Record the number of hours from your Project Log.

_____ hours

4. Now that you have worked on the project for a while, do you think you can finish it independently?

☐ I am sure I will finish.
☐ I'll finish, but I may need some help.
☐ I'll need lots of help!

I will need help with:

_____

_____

_____

continued on next page. . .

133

5. Below is a list of problems students working on a project sometimes encounter. Check each item that identifies an area where you might need help. (If you don't think you need any help at all, check the last item.)

- ☐ I can't find enough information about my topic.
- ☐ I don't have enough time to work on the project.
- ☐ I'm having trouble making myself work on the project.
- ☐ This project is more difficult than I thought it would be.
- ☐ It isn't possible to do some of the things I planned to do.

I need help to:

- ☐ write a report
- ☐ design a poster or other visuals
- ☐ make a presentation
- ☐ organize my work into a display
- ☐ conduct independent research
- ☐ decide when I've done enough work

- ☐ I am doing quite well and I don't need any help.

6. If you have other problems or questions, list them here.

_____

_____

_____

_____

_____

_____

_____

_____

_____

_____

_____

Interview Checklist

STUDENT NAME

Setting Up the Interview

☐ Find someone with expertise in your subject area. (Check with teachers, family members, the Yellow Pages for ideas.)

☐ Write, call, or e-mail to set up an appointment for the interview.

☐ Identify yourself and explain why you want an interview.

☐ Let your expert know what (if anything) he or she needs to prepare for the interview.

☐ Schedule enough time to get your questions answered.

☐ Get permission to audiotape or videotape the interview.

☐ Record the name, title, and contact information of the person you'll be interviewing.

☐ Confirm the appointment date, time, and place.

☐ Thank your expert for agreeing to the interview.

Before the Interview

☐ Prepare your questions. Think about your audience and what they might want to know, and avoid questions that can simply be answered "yes" or "no." Remember to ask a lot of "why" questions. Along with the specific questions you want to ask, write a few warm-up questions. (You may want to ask your supervising teacher to review your questions.)

☐ Confirm the appointment date, time, and place, and make sure to inform your parent or guardian and supervising teacher to get their permission.

During the Interview

☐ Arrive on time or a little bit early.

☐ Dress appropriately, and bring everything you'll need: paper, writing utensils, recording equipment, camera and film, etc.

☐ Thank your expert for agreeing to the interview.

☐ Act interested and enthusiastic.

☐ Start with your warm-up questions.

☐ Follow up with your specific questions.

☐ Listen carefully, and ask for clarification if you need to.

☐ Stay within the time limit you agreed on. Go over only if your expert says it's okay.

☐ Offer to show your expert a copy of your interview summary for review. This will allow your expert to correct any misunderstanding.

☐ Thank your expert again at the end of the interview.

After the Interview

☐ Write up your summary as soon as possible while your conversation is fresh.

☐ Write your expert a thank-you note.

Adapted from *School Power: Strategies for Succeeding in School* by Jeanne Shay Schumm, Ph.D., and Marguerite Radencich, Ph.D. © 1992 by Jeanne Shay Schumm, and Marguerite Radencich. Reprinted by permission of Free Spirit Publishing, Minneapolis, MN. 1-800-735-7323. *www.freespirit.com*

Giving Oral Presentations

STUDENT NAME

While there are always those people who seem right at home talking in front of a crowd, most people need lots of practice to become skilled public speakers. Even the most seasoned speakers sometimes feel jitters and nerves, so you're in good company. Don't worry about being perfect. Just do the best you can and minimize potential problems through preparation and practice.

Preparing to Present

☐ Organize your presentation the same way you'd organize a written paper. Think about your audience, topic, purpose, and format. Include an introduction, explanation, and conclusion.

☐ Brainstorm power-packed openers and closing statements. These are the parts of your presentation listeners will remember most.

☐ Time yourself. Stick to the time limit you've targeted.

☐ Include examples, stories, facts, and even jokes.

☐ Use visuals you've developed: charts, graphs, illustrations, etc. Be sure to practice using them ahead of time so you won't fumble during your presentation.

☐ If you don't feel comfortable giving your presentation from memory, try speaking from an outline on index cards.

☐ Appearances count. Dress appropriately on the day of your presentation. (And remember, how you dress may depend on your audience and your presentation itself!)

If You'll Be Going Solo. . .

☐ Think about who you like to listen to speak and who you don't. Try to figure out what they do that makes you feel this way. Use your observations to plan your own presentation.

☐ Practice giving your speech in front of a mirror. This will help you see what your audience will be seeing.

☐ Practice saying your speech into a tape recorder and listen to it. Are you going too fast? Too slow? Are you mumbling? Is there a particular part that needs more work? Do you sound excited?

If You'll Be Presenting with a Group. . .

☐ Make sure each group member recognizes his or her responsibilities. Write down all of the report-related group responsibilities and assign them to individual group members.

☐ Practice with your group members, using time limits. Afterward, share suggestions and practice again.

☐ Practice with visuals and props. For example, you might want one group member to hold up a poster during the presentation. Rehearse this in advance so you don't waste time sorting things out in front of your audience.

 Adapted from *School Power: Strategies for Succeeding in School* by Jeanne Shay Schumm, Ph.D., and Marguerite Radencich, Ph.D. © 1992 by Jeanne Shay Schumm, and Marguerite Radencich. Reprinted by permission of Free Spirit Publishing, Minneapolis, MN. 1-800-735-7323. *www.freespirit.com*

Program Evaluation Form

STUDENT NAME

Please give us your opinions on *Challenging Projects for Creative Minds*. Be honest and specific in all of your answers to the questions below. Ask a parent to look at the form with you and offer suggestions. We are interested in parent responses, too. Have a parent sign the evaluation before you turn it in.

1. How would you rate the difficulty of the project you have just completed?

☐ Too easy

☐ Sort of challenging

☐ Very challenging

☐ Too hard

Comments: _____

_____

_____

_____

2. How well do you think the program is organized?

☐ Poorly organized

☐ Okay, but could be better

☐ Well organized

☐ Very well organized

What did you like or what improvements can you suggest:

_____

_____

_____

_____

3. Did your supervising teacher offer help and encouragement when you needed it?

☐ No, very rarely

☐ Sometimes, but not enough

☐ Occasionally, and it was usually enough

☐ Yes, plenty

Please give examples: _____

_____

_____

_____

4. Do you feel that you gained anything of personal value from the project?

☐ No, nothing

☐ A little

☐ Yes, quite a bit

☐ Yes, very much

Please give examples: _____

_____

_____

_____

continued on next page. . .

5. Did you enjoy working on this project?

☐ No, not at all
☐ A little
☐ Yes, quite a bit
☐ Yes, very much

What was it that made the project enjoyable or not enjoyable?

_____

_____

_____

_____

6. If another student asked you about *Challenging Projects for Creative Minds,* what would you say? Would you advise a friend to work on a project? Why or why not?

_____

_____

_____

_____

7. What suggestions can you give to improve the program (not the project you worked on, but the program itself)?

_____

_____

_____

_____

8. Taking everything into account (difficulty, organization, explanations of what you were expected to do, the amount of help and encouragement provided by your supervising teacher, the value of the project to you personally, etc.), how would you rate the program?

On a scale from 1 – 5, I think the *Challenging Projects for Creative Minds* program is:

☐ 5 Excellent
☐ 4 Good
☐ 3 Okay
☐ 2 Only fair
☐ 1 Not worth the effort

Student signature: _____   Date: _____

Parent or guardian signature: _____   Date: _____

Forms for Teachers

Outcomes Form

Project Title: _____

Before you begin writing the assignment, determine what outcomes you want students to achieve. Ask, Why are we doing this? What results are we looking for? What will students learn? In the spaces below, record three or four significant learner outcomes that will result from the project you are developing. These can be outcomes established by your school district or goals you have for your students.

Learner Outcomes

1. _____
_____
_____
_____
_____

2. _____
_____
_____
_____
_____

3. _____
_____
_____
_____
_____

4. _____
_____
_____
_____
_____

Keep these outcomes in mind as you write the project.

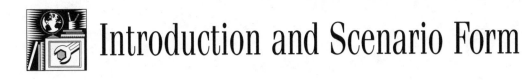
Introduction and Scenario Form

Project Title: _____

Introduction:

What does the project allow students to do?

_____

_____

_____

_____

Project Scenario: The project scenario contains four parts:

Role. What role will students play as they work on the project?

Assignment. What will the students' tasks be in this role?

Products. What tangible products will students create or develop?

Demonstration. How will students demonstrate or present their work?

Be sure to include all four aspects in the scenario you write:

_____

_____

_____

_____

_____

_____

_____

_____

_____

_____

_____

_____

_____

_____

_____

_____

Assignment Form

Project Title: _____

Develop the assignment by writing project requirements in a logical order of progression. What must students do to successfully complete the project? Describe each component of the project as an assignment step. As you work on your draft, remember that the assignment should make sense within the context of the scenario that you've written. Begin each step with an active verb.

To complete this project successfully students will:

1. _____
   _____

2. _____
   _____

3. _____
   _____

4. _____
   _____

5. _____
   _____

6. _____
   _____

7. _____
   _____

8. _____
   _____

9. _____
   _____

10. _____
   _____

Assessment Form

STUDENT NAME

Project Title: _____

Student Responsibilities

1. _____
2. _____
3. _____
4. _____
5. _____
6. _____
7. _____

ASSESSMENT SCALE

4 Exceeded Expectations

3 Achieved Expectations

2 Needs Time to Achieve Expectations

1 Showed Little or No Evidence that Expectations were Achieved

	SELF	TEACHER	OTHER

PROCESS

1. _____
2. _____
3. _____
4. _____
5. _____
6. _____
7. _____
8. _____
9. _____
10. _____

PRODUCTS

11. _____
12. _____
13. _____
14. _____
15. _____
16. _____
17. _____
18. _____
19. _____
20. _____

CONTENT

21. _____
22. _____
23. _____
24. _____
25. _____
26. _____
27. _____
28. _____
29. _____
30. _____

Written Comments Form

STUDENT NAME

Project Title: _____

Use this form to keep notes on positive aspects of a student's work throughout the course of a project. Give specific examples of what you observed, and include these notes with your assessment of the project.

Motivation: _____
_____
_____

Setting personal goals: _____
_____
_____

Creativity: _____
_____
_____

Problem solving: _____
_____
_____

Decision making: _____
_____
_____

Self-reflection: _____
_____
_____

Other: _____
_____
_____

Basics for Success Form

Project Title: _____

What skills and knowledge do students need to complete this project successfully? Look at the assignment carefully, and list the basic prerequisites in the column on the left. For example, to make attractive posters, students need to measure and mark straight lines on posterboard or have desktop publishing skills and equipment capable of creating the desired effects.

    Then answer the questions in the right-hand columns with a Y (yes) or N (no): Is it reasonable to expect students to use this skill? Have students mastered the necessary skills? Will you have to teach a lesson on, for example, measuring and drawing lines to prepare students? Based on your answers to these questions, you can determine the specific skills or knowledge that you will teach or model to prepare students for this project.

	BASIC SKILLS OR KNOWLEDGE	IS IT REASONABLE TO EXPECT THIS SKILL?	HAVE STUDENTS MASTERED THIS SKILL?	WILL PRETEACHING OR MODELING BE NECESSARY?
1.				
2.				
3.				
4.				
5.				
6.				
7.				
8.				
9.				
10.				

Expectations Form

Project Title: _____

Because student performance is assessed in terms of whether or not students have met the expectations for the project, it's important to define the expectations very clearly. In the spaces below describe your expectations for each item on the Assessment Form. Be as specific as possible. The language you use will establish a basis for assessment, so it should not be the least ambiguous or vague. It should provide measurable standards that students can understand and strive to achieve. Getting student input on the expectations can be very valuable. The more students are involved in setting the expectations, the more likely they are to strive to meet them.

Requirement: _____
Expectation: _____
_____
_____

Requirement: _____
Expectation: _____
_____
_____

Requirement: _____
Expectation: _____
_____
_____

Requirement: _____
Expectation: _____
_____
_____

Requirement: _____
Expectation: _____
_____
_____

Certificate of Completion

Awarded to _____

School District _____

School _____   **Grade** _____

Date _____

This is to certify that the above-named student has satisfactorily completed the Creative Minds project

The student has exceeded the requirements of the regular curriculum and demonstrated independence and persistence.

We, the undersigned, wish to congratulate you on your accomplishment. You have shown motivation, independence, and academic achievement.

_____
Supervising Teacher

_____
Principal

Certificate of Merit

Awarded to _____

Date _____

School District _____

Grade _____

School _____

This is to certify that the above-named student has completed, with a high degree of excellence,

the Creative Minds project _____

★ Congratulations! ★

We, the undersigned, salute your extraordinary academic achievement. You have demonstrated exceptional ability in the creation and presentation of your project. Your willingness and determination to strive beyond the basic curriculum will serve you well in today's world.

_____
Superintendent of Schools

_____
Principal

_____
Supervising Teacher

From *Challenging Projects for Creative Minds* by Phil Schlemmer, M.Ed., and Dori Schlemmer © 1999. Free Spirit Publishing Inc., Minneapolis, MN; 800/735-7323; www.freespirit.com. This page may be photocopied for individual, classroom, or group work only.

Resources

BIBLIOGRAPHY

Armstrong, Thomas. *Multiple Intelligences in the Classroom.* Alexandria, VA: Association for Supervision and Curriculum Development, 1994.

Branscomb, H. Eric. *Casting Your Net: A Student's Guide to Research on the Internet.* Needham Heights, MA: Allyn & Bacon, 1997.

Chapman, Carolyn. *If the Shoe Fits: How to Develop Multiple Intelligences in the Classroom.* Palantine, IL: IRI SkyLight Publishing, 1993.

Slavin, Robert. "Ability Grouping, Cooperative Learning, and the Gifted." *Journal for the Education of the Gifted* 14:1 (Fall 1990): 3–8.

Gardner, Howard. *Frames of Mind: The Theory of Multiple Intelligences.* New York: Basic Books, 1993.

Jensen, Eric. *Introduction to Brain-Compatible Learning.* San Diego, CA: The Brain Store, 1998.

Johnson, David W., Roger T. Johnson, and Edythe J. Holubec. *Cooperation in the Classroom* (6th edition). Alexandria, VA: Association for Supervision and Curriculum Development, 1994.

Lewis, Barbara A. *The Kid's Guide to Service Projects: Over 500 Service Ideas for Young People Who Want to Make a Difference.* Minneapolis: Free Spirit Publishing, 1996.

Schlemmer, Phil. "A Learning-to-Learn Curriculum Model." *Changing Schools* (October 1995): 8–9.

————. "Curriculum Development: Quality Education in a Budget-Cutting Age." *Illinois School Research and Development.* (Fall 1981): 22–26.

————. *Learning on Your Own.* New York: The Center for Applied Research in Education, 1987. (A five-volume series).

Shulman, Judith H., Rachel A. Lotan, and Jennifer A. Whitcomb. *Groupwork in Diverse Classrooms: A Casebook for Educators.* New York: Teachers College Press, 1998.

Schumm, Jeanne Shay, and Marguerite Radencich. *School Power: Strategies for Succeeding in School.* Minneapolis: Free Spirit Publishing, 1992.

Winebrenner, Susan. *Teaching Gifted Kids in the Regular Classroom: Strategies and Techniques Every Teacher Can Use to Meet the Academic Needs of the Gifted and Talented.* Minneapolis: Free Spirit Publishing, 1992.

————. *Teaching Kids with Learning Difficulties in the Regular Classroom: Strategies and Techniques Every Teacher Can Use to Challenge & Motivate Struggling Students.* Free Spirit Publishing, 1996.

STUDENT RESOURCES

The Complete Idiot's Guide to Speaking in Public with Confidence by Laurie E. Rozakis. (Topanga, CA: AlphaBooks, 1996). This guide is packed with solid information, tips, and warnings that help people build the skills for delivering winning speeches and presentations.

Get Off My Brain by Randall McCutcheon. (Minneapolis: Free Spirit Publishing, 1998). This survival guide for students who are bored, frustrated, and otherwise sick of school helps readers sharpen their skills, speak up in class, and improve their GPA with less effort.

An Incomplete Education by Judy Jones and William Wilson. (New York: Ballantine, 1995). This book provides a solid overview of a wide range of disciplines from American studies, to art history, economics, film, literature, music, philosophy, political science, psychology, science, and more.

The Essential Researcher: A Complete, Up-to-Date, One-Volume Sourcebook for Journalists, Writers, Students, and Everyone Who Needs Facts Fast by Maureen Croteau and Wayne Worcester. (New York: Harper Collins, 1993). This is a quick and handy research guide packed with information on a tremendous number of topics.

Get Organized by Rod Fry. (Franklin Lakes, NJ: Career Press, 1996). This book is a great resource on time management for students. It can help them set goals, stay on track, and study smarter.

Talking About People: A Guide to Fair and Accurate Language by Rosalie Maggio. (Phoenix, AZ: Oryx Press, 1997). The author offers thousands of alternatives to help writers and speakers avoid oudated and stereotypical language.

The Ultimate Visual Dictionary of Science. (New York: Dorling Kindersly Publishing, 1997). The bright graphics in this book make science come alive. Covering a broad range of science topics from astronomy to zoology, this reference book makes difficult concepts clear through illustrations, cross-sections, diagrams, and photographs.

A Writer's Companion: A Handy Compendium of Useful but Hard-to-Find Information on History, Literature, Art, Sciece, Travel, Philosophy and Much More edited by Jerry Leath Mills and Louis D. Rubin (New York: Harper Collins, 1997). This reference book collects a wealth of information not readily found in dictionaries, almanacs, or encyclopedias.

Index

About the Authors

Phil Schlemmer, M.Ed., has been a teacher, writer, consultant, and curriculum designer since 1973. He currently works in the Holland Public School District in Holland, Michigan, helping to implement innovative instructional strategies. His work focuses on teaching students how to become self-directed, lifelong learners. He has previously published six books and many professional articles.

In addition to helping her husband, Phil, write hundreds of projects that promote self-directed learning, **Dori Schlemmer** has created specialized curriculum materials for local school districts since 1976. She currently works for the Kentwood Public School district in Grand Rapids, Michigan. Her work at the high school focuses on providing school-to-career opportunities, training, and resources for students and staff.

Phil and Dori live in Kentwood, Michigan, with their daughter, Erin.

Other Great Books from Free Spirit

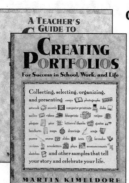

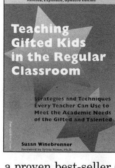